Mama Needs a Do-Over

"Too often we want to throw in the towel when we face hard days in motherhood. Lisa's words will inspire you, as a mother, to view your problems as potential sources for positive spiritual change, and her laugh-out-loud humor will give your heart the joy it needs."

Amber Lia, television and film producer,
founder and writer of MotherOfKnights.com

"If laughter truly is medicine for the soul, then we all need a huge dose of Lisa Pennington's honesty about resetting our lives. Her book is filled with hope and practical solutions for making lemonade out of some of the lemons in our day. I laughed my way through her book and am inspired to live above my circumstances by hitting my reset button before things get ugly. Thank you, Lisa!"

Roxanne Parks, founder and president
of Winter Summit Ministries, Inc.

mama
needs
* a *
do-over

mama
needs
a
do-over

SIMPLE STEPS
TO TURNING A
HARD DAY AROUND

Lisa Pennington

transforming lives together

MAMA NEEDS A DO-OVER
Published by David C Cook
4050 Lee Vance View
Colorado Springs, CO 80918 U.S.A.

David C Cook Distribution Canada
55 Woodslee Avenue, Paris, Ontario, Canada N3L 3E5

David C Cook U.K., Kingsway Communications
Eastbourne, East Sussex BN23 6NT, England

The graphic circle C logo is a registered trademark of David C Cook.

All Scripture quotations are taken from the Holy Bible, New International
Version®, NIV®. Copyright © 1973, 2011 by Biblica, Inc.® Used by permission
of Zondervan. All rights reserved worldwide. www.zondervan.com.

LCCN 2015944631
ISBN 978-0-7814-1292-6
eISBN 978-0-7814-1366-4

Published in association with the literacy agency of D. C. Jacobson &
Associates LLC, an Author Management Company. www.dcjacobson.com

The Team: Ingrid Beck, Nicci Hubert, Amy Konyndyk,
Nick Lee, Tiffany Thomas, Karen Athen
Cover Design: Faceout Studio, Derek Thornton

Printed in the United States of America
First Edition 2015

1 2 3 4 5 6 7 8 9 10

062915

To my amazing husband, James, and
our nine beautiful children.
I love each of you to the ends of the earth and back.

Contents

Welcome

I tend to get myself into messes. I don't know why I am such a magnet for finding myself in a pickle, but it's frequent and funny. Almost every day I will lose something or drop something or forget an appointment. The good news is that I have never left a child somewhere ... so far—knock on wood.

But even with all of my *I Love Lucy* adventures, I truly enjoy life. If I had to wait for perfection before I have a good time, I'd be too old and hard of hearing to appreciate it.

Awhile back I shared a post on my blog called "20 Ways to Reset When the Kids Are Having a Hard Day." It went viral! I realized I had hit on something that tired moms needed to hear ... that there is a way out of those desperate moments, and the key is YOU. And it's about more than just surviving. This is about true, deep, life-changing joy that can spring from those awful moments.

We all have areas of weakness, and if we don't laugh at ourselves, the only thing we have left is anger and irritation. I've found that my shortcomings are an opportunity for me to learn. For instance, I always pin my skirt to my Spanx before leaving the house. Don't ask me what led to my learning that little trick. But it involves a giant mirror and a shopping cart.

With nine children that we homeschool and a husband who works from home, there is a lot of opportunity for laughing and learning around here. Add to that my desire to remodel the kitchen rather than actually cook in it and we are a constant flow of mishaps and adventures.

God is right there in the middle of it all. He is so full of mercy and generosity and grace that He fills in all of the gaps that my flaws leave behind. Mothering has been, without a doubt, the hardest project I ever took on. But the good news is that even though I fail over and over again in my efforts to do it completely perfectly, He fixes it for me. He covers my mistakes. He teaches my kids. He carries us all.

And my messes remind me that I am not always so easy to be around. When I get huffy (yes, I can get in a huff occasionally) about things not going my way, I am reminded of the trouble I created last week for my poor husband or the time I disciplined my son for something he didn't do. #motherguilt

And I want to crawl into my bed—at ten o'clock in the morning—and not get up.

That's where so many of us are. In a place of hurt and depression and hopelessness.

We all have hard days, and sometimes we have hard years. For me the past year, as I wrote this book, was a doozy! There were many days when I wondered how I would get from morning to night without falling apart. My list of tough lessons, mistakes, losses, and painful moments is too long to go into. But before we both start crying, let me tell you the good news. Like Dorothy as she found her way back home, I had the power all along. But instead of going to Kansas, I was heading straight to true joy! Through my relationship with Christ and the gifts that He gave me, this mama got to have plenty of do-overs.

And that's where we begin this book. With fears and doubts and messes all around that we wonder if we can ever recover from. We'll meet in my kitchen for some hot tea and laughter.

I want to encourage you that while you may not be able to pull off the kind of perfection that you want (in fact, you definitely can't), God sees your heart. He says it is just the way He designed it to be. Beautiful, talented, dreamy, capable, and strong.

It starts with you. Right where you are.

And we will let go of perfection ... just toss that sucker right out the window. When I visit friends they will often apologize for the condition of their home. "Oh, it's a mess in there ... please don't look," or, "I have been meaning to repaint this room; the walls are filthy!" My friend, please don't do that. It doesn't matter one bit if your house isn't perfect. In the words of Elsa, let it go! We all have messy spots in our lives, and while we might need to clean them up, they don't define us. I'm not embarrassed about my dusty bookshelves and you shouldn't be either. This book is a perfect-free zone.

Insecurities can get in the way of really opening up and letting yourself be seen. Or they can make you feel like the other person expects something from you. I promise you, there is none of that here. It's just you and me and these pages. We can cast off all of those burdens and just be real. I'll show you my messy closet and I'll ask that you don't hide your junk drawer. Then we can relax and learn and grow together.

God says in 2 Timothy 2:15 that He approves of us! He created us, and when we start to doubt our worth and think that we can't do anything well, we are doubting the beauty of His creation. He made you wonderfully and desires that you appreciate what He gave you. He especially desires that you don't try to be someone you're not meant to be. We can't know why He made us the way He did, but we can trust that in His infinite wisdom He meant us to be this way. He meant for me to fall in love with the giant chalkboard in my kitchen, and I know He meant you to love the things that you love.

In these pages I want to remind you of who you are in Christ and who you can be with your kids. I'll help you find that hopeful girl you used to be so you can believe in yourself again. There will be a few simple assignments after each chapter. These will require paper and pencil, but you don't have to stress about them. You don't even have to be right in your answers! Just write what comes to mind. You can use a pencil if you want to erase and change as you go. But I'm going to be daring and write mine with a pen. Maybe even a Sharpie! Don't be scared … it's not much. Ain't nobody got time for homework.

I've also included wisdom from many other books that have influenced my life. I hope you love them as much as I do.

At the end of the book is a whole slew of ideas to get you started in finding that joyful place you are searching for. It isn't intended for you to copy exactly but to ignite ideas in you that are even better than mine! And you will notice that I don't use any electronics or video games as I seek ways to help my kids turn hard days into fun. That's very purposeful. Electronics are just a Band-Aid and end up creating more problems. Let's leave those for just occasional fun and not include them in our solutions to getting through a difficult time.

There's so much in you that is amazing. Come with me through a journey of hope and joy and humor that will lead you to a place of victory and a fresh beginning.

Right where you are.

Get ready for a do-over.

CHAPTER 1

Knowing Yourself

Therefore we do not lose heart. Though outwardly
we are wasting away, yet inwardly we are being
renewed day by day. For our light and momentary
troubles are achieving for us an eternal glory that
far outweighs them all. So we fix our eyes not on
what is seen, but on what is unseen, since what is
seen is temporary, but what is unseen is eternal.
(2 Cor. 4:16–18)

I just love my kitchen. It's bright and cheery and fills my need to be
surrounded by aqua and white. Fourteen years ago, when we bought
our ninety-year-old, small Texas farmhouse, the kitchen had no place
for a dishwasher, no pantry, no counter space, and the refrigerator
literally just sat in the middle of the floor.

My son and I tackled the remodel project together. I spent weeks
sketching out ideas and picking colors and searching for deals on
building materials and appliances. Our budget was very small, so I
did all of the work myself. It was then that I discovered my love for
using power tools. Every morning when I woke up, I would get all

excited that I was going to be able to play with my compound miter saw that had laser cutting precision. In fact, for Valentine's Day that year, my husband bought me a pancake air compressor with a brad nailer. It was very romantic.

It was through that huge remodel project that I discovered I am pretty good at simple woodworking. I taught myself how to add all kinds of trim to my cheap off-the-rack cabinets to make them look like custom cabinetry. My newly discovered talent gave my little budget kitchen an upgrade that I could not have afforded otherwise.

I really wanted to do the kitchen right, so we ripped everything out, including the floor and ceiling. I remember every few hours sitting in the corner nursing my baby and wiping Sheetrock dust off of his precious little head. Good times.

It took vision and stepping out in faith to totally gut my kitchen with almost no experience. I was naive and I believed I could do it. But of course, ripping out was the easy part. Then I had to put it all back together again. In the six weeks that we worked on it, I never lost my confidence. Even though I sometimes had to spend hours figuring out how to do the simplest thing, I was able to see in my mind the finished room throughout the whole grueling process. That kept me going.

Being able to see a vision for a room is something I learned early in my life that I have a knack for. I can tell if a piece of furniture will fit in a certain spot before I buy it, what will look good against a wall, what kinds of window coverings will enhance the space, things like that. My friends often ask me to come to their house and look at their room to help them figure out a new arrangement or solve a problem. I don't know why I can do that, but it comes easily to me. I don't take credit for it. I know for sure that God gave me that gift.

If we were chatting over coffee, I might ask you these questions: Are you a sports girl? Are you a closet *Real Housewives* watcher? Do you consider yourself to be an expert in anything? Do you want to be an expert in something? How do you spend most of your time? What would you buy with an extra hundred dollars? What were the last five books you read just for yourself? Who are the three people you admire most? Inquiring minds want to know.

What are your best and worst qualities? Many of my qualities fall on both sides of the line. I can get obsessive about things. BAD. But that makes me a person who gets things done. GOOD. I can't cook. BAD. But that gives my kids an opportunity to grow beyond me and teach me. GOOD.

Even though we don't get to sit together, there are a few things I already know about you. Your family is everything to you, your kids are amazing, and you have good days and some really rotten days.

It's universal to all moms … amazing kids and rotten days. No one loves the stinky stuff. We all go through seasons that seem like more bad than good. It's part of life. And when your kids are really young it can feel like the days of cleaning up potty messes and taking half an hour just to get buckled into the minivan will drag on forever. They won't. I promise.

A book that inspires me to accept the hard days is *Mended: Pieces of a Life Made Whole* by Angie Smith. Angie has a great perspective on today: "We need not dwell on the things we wish we had done differently, nor should we even give too much thought to what the future will look like. We need not worry about the complete picture, but rather the fact that we have this moment. Right now. And I want to make it count."[1]

But we have to start here ... with you ... and get to the nitty-gritty of who you are.

WHAT ARE YOU GOOD AT?

We all have abilities that are easier for us than for most people. I know there are things you can do that I would practically bow at your feet if I could watch you. It's such a treat to be around others when they are using the gifts God gave them. It's like seeing His brilliance in action.

The phrase "Each with his own gift" became so obvious one day when we were having our septic tank pumped. It seemed like a disgusting job to me, but the man who was doing it was a genius in the ways of tanks and pumps and all things related to potties that he brought it to life. He was so passionate about his job that my children and I stood around his giant hose, riveted to his every word as he explained the process of taking excellent care of our septic system. He inspired us to be better flushers. What a gift!

It's a beautiful thing, knowing your strengths and being able to use them in your daily life. And it sounds so easy, doesn't it? But I find that people struggle to answer the simple question, "What are you good at?" It always surprises me that they hem and haw and don't know what to say. Whether they are being humble or actually can't think of an answer is hard to tell. We seem to struggle with announcing our talents as if it is being prideful.

But we need to know. God gave each of us special gifts that we are supposed to be using. Joseph, in the book of Genesis, could interpret dreams. What would have happened if he had been shy about that? He might have stayed in prison, and his family could have starved. The lineage of Christ was on the line!

It's important to understand yourself so that you can become the person you were created to be. There is, without a doubt, a long list of things you are good at. So let's take a look at those. What gifts did God give you?

Some gifts we become aware of early on, like if we are musical or athletic. But sometimes we find out things later in life, like my woodworking skills for example. I didn't discover that until I was in my late thirties. You have amazing abilities that I could never dream of having. You are unique and so, so, so special. You probably have some of the same talents that a few of your friends have. But you can't be exactly like anyone else. We are not supposed to be alike and we shouldn't try to be.

In the parable of the talents, the master gave each servant a different amount of talents. To one he gave five, another two, and another one, each according to his abilities. God is handing us talents and goals every day. Wouldn't it be nice to know what those are and what to do with them? I sure don't want to be like the servant who buried his talent because he was afraid to lose it. I want to double what God gave me!

As you think about the abilities you have to tap into, you can use them not only to serve others but also to help yourself through difficulties. So I want you to mull it over. Ask yourself, "What am I good at?" There are tests you can take to determine your spiritual gifts and personality strengths, and that might be a good idea if you have never done that. But for now, let's keep it simple. Just say whatever pops into your head.

My first thought probably wouldn't be something deep. I'd just toss out whatever relates to my life lately. I might say, "I am good at choosing perfect avocados." That is a special gift, by the way. There are few things in life better than a really good avocado. God can definitely use my avocado-choosing ability for good!

Start paying attention throughout the day to what comes easily to you. It doesn't matter how insignificant it may seem.

WHAT DO YOU LOVE?

Another way to figure out your gifts is by answering this easy question: What kinds of things do you love? I, being a passionate person, love many things. I love my husband and my nine kids, our little house, my friends, the giant chalkboard in my kitchen. I could go on and on.

And if I love something I will give my whole heart to it. I'd throw myself onto train tracks to save my iPhone. And if I didn't have a frugal husband who protects our finances like the queen's guards at Buckingham Palace, I would go into debt buying every color of destruction-proof phone cases. He, however, loves keeping our money all neat and tidy and out of my hands. Being careful and budgety and having receipts organized makes him happy. (This, I am convinced, is something God finds entertaining because I am receipt challenged, so putting the two of us together must really give Him a chuckle.)

If you and I were sitting together right now and I asked you, "What do you love?" what would you say? I would want to hear all about your quirky collections and your coffee obsession and what TV shows you refuse to miss a single episode of.

I remember once hearing a preacher say that if he wanted to get to know someone he would ask who his five closest friends are. Interesting. If I want to get to know someone I ask what her five favorite things are. I want to see how she lives and where she relaxes and what she keeps on her bedside table. The table by my bed, for instance, has three books waiting to be read that have been sitting there for over a year, my iPhone charger, some peppermint lip balm, and a green construction paper box that my son made for me when he was five (he is now twenty-three). Those six items would tell you this about me: that I really want to read but I don't find the time, I like to stay fully charged, I am addicted to lip balm, and I wish my kids could stay little forever. That pretty much sums me up.

Quick. Name five things on your bedside table. Or on your desk. Or in your purse. Or wherever you keep your personal stuff. It might just say a lot about who you are at the very heart.

If I asked you to tell me your five favorite physical objects in your home, what would they be? I'm not going to tell anyone, so just blurt it out. My things might look pretty shallow to you. I mean, I should probably say the kids' baby pictures and the oil painting I inherited from my grandmother. But it would be more likely that first I'd say the fuzzy blanket on my bed. No answer is right or wrong here.

Now ask yourself, "What does this say about me?" I'm not looking for godly answers. I just want you to see yourself for who you are and get in touch with what it is that makes your heart go pitter pat. My phone, for example. I know it's just a "thing." But my phone does occasionally just make me smile when I see it sitting next to me. And it's not all superficial. My phone is something I saved money for and sacrificed to buy. It helps me stay in touch with my kids and remember appointments. I keep my health journal there, and it allows me to snap a picture of my kids that I would have missed if I had to go get the big-girl camera every time. It gives me worship music when I am exercising and helps me manage my Etsy shop. It's awesome in so many ways. And yes, I do play games on it sometimes. Mama needs to unwind occasionally.

Whatever you have near you right now and whatever it is that you just adore for no explainable reason are things that say a lot about you. It really is the simple things in life that bring us the most pleasure.

WHAT ARE YOUR WEAKNESSES?

While we are taking a look at what we love, let's be sure to take a glance at our weaknesses too. I know … ouch, right? But it is so good to be able to see where you need help! I have definitely got issues. For example, I struggle to understand technology. Like, STRUGGLE. I have spent endless hours in Google searching things like, "How to change your profile picture in Facebook," and "How do I turn on the Wii before my kids figure out I don't know anything?!" Technology is my Kryptonite even though I have to use it every day.

It has helped me so much in my life to appreciate my weaknesses. I can't expect myself to be able to do everything well. If we could all be strong in every area, why would we need each other? My kids get a thrill when they have to help me figure out something techie that is *so* simple to them. They think it's so funny that I can't figure it out.

I love being able to help a friend (that would go on my "things I love to do" list for sure!) and I couldn't do that if no one ever let me see their struggles. Sometimes we need to work on those weak areas. We can always improve. But generally speaking those will always be things we have to work harder on.

Emily P. Freeman (my daughters especially love her) in her book *Grace for the Good Girl* really sums up the way of Christ in our weakness:

> For the girl who wears the mask of strength and responsibility, it is important to explore her perceptions of weakness. Consider what Jesus says about weakness. He chose the foolish things of the world to shame the wise and the weak things of the world to shame the strong (1 Cor. 1:27). It doesn't make sense to me and it isn't the way I'd have done it. But it is the way of Jesus.[2]

Our weaknesses define us as much as our strengths do. Embrace them! Let them grow you and mature you. Some weaknesses are harder to admit than others. My struggle with food, for example. It will be a lifelong battle for me and it can be embarrassing (so much that I want to eat a half gallon of ice cream in shame), but if I will see it as something I can learn from I might actually see a way I can use it to improve my life. And ask for help! It takes a wise woman to be able to see when she needs to ask for help and allow someone else to be better than she is at something. What a gift you give to your friend when you let her teach you or help you. Even if it is in a small way, we need one another like that.

WHAT SURROUNDS YOU?

There is a lot to be learned about a person by seeing her surroundings. I don't mean how clean you are or if you've made the bed today. That doesn't matter at all to me. I am sure you want to keep it tidy and organized, so let's just look past all of that. Even if you're neat, it's not always going to be perfect. Neatness doesn't tell me anything about you that I really want to know (unless you're OCD about it; then I am fascinated).

If you look around the room of your house that you are in right now (if you're not at home then wait till later ... whatever is at Starbucks doesn't count!) what do you see? Are there things there that you don't like? Do you have too much stuff? Is there a lamp that you got from Aunt Martha as a wedding gift that you can't figure out how to part with even though you really can't stand it? That says to me that you are tender, which is a good quality when used wisely.

I have a lot of junk furniture that I painted or altered in some way. I move things around. A LOT. (Hello, my name is Lisa and I'm a rearrange-aholic.) I am surrounded by art that my kids made, Bible verses, uplifting quotes, and lots of Mason jars filled with anything from plants to lights to dead leaves. If I were to examine myself by my surroundings I'd say I love vintage because it reminds me of the good old days, I like to show my kids that I treasure them by keeping their "masterpieces" on display, and I crave creativity, which is why I make furniture instead of buying it new.

Like your bedside table, what surrounds you speaks volumes. And the good news is that if you are trying to change something about yourself, you can also change the stuff you have around you. In fact, you can do that so much more easily that it might be where you decide to start. Get rid of that lamp to start with! And if decorating is not your thing, ask a friend to come over and help. Then offer to help her with whatever you are good at in exchange.

THE GIRL WHO SPARKLES

You know, my son was only nine years old when he and I remodeled the kitchen together. One job that we had to tackle was to install a layer of plywood over the entire floor. We had to use these mammoth-sized nails and put one every four inches in a grid over the whole surface. Don't ask me why. I just did what the guy at the hardware store told me combined with what I saw on HGTV.

I gave my son a hammer and told him that I would start each nail and then he could follow after me and pound them the rest of the way in.

After only a few nails (we had to put about three hundred nails in the floor) I saw that my plan wasn't going to work. He couldn't hammer hard enough to get the nails all the way down. In fact, he could barely get them partway. Then they would start to bend, causing me to have to pull the nail back out and … well … you get the picture.

I thought about it. He obviously wasn't good at hammering the nails in, but what was he good at? This kid loved math problems, so I took the hammer from him and gave him a measuring tape and pencil instead. "Honey, why don't you make a mark every four inches all over the floor and I will hammer a nail in on each mark?"

He looked around and walked over to a pile of wood scraps. He picked up a four inch strip of plywood and held it out to me. "Mom, why don't we just use this to mark a grid all over the floor and then you can put a nail at each place the lines meet?"

Well, duh! Why hadn't I thought of that?

He spent the next half hour making lines like a pro while I started hammering.

We had tapped into his gift, and he came up with a simple, beautiful idea that not only worked really well but also built his confidence.

Of course, it wasn't perfect because I had to pound every nail in myself. My arms, twelve years later, are still sore.

Some days we wonder where those talents of ours, the gifts we have that used to be so much a part of us, went. Motherhood is hard, y'all. Our gifts can seem to have been washed away by years of being late for church every single week and never being able to find … well … anything. Where did that girl go who was so good at keeping her car clean? Remember her? She always looked so cute.

She is there. She may be hidden or seem lost forever, but we are going to get her back. It will definitely be a more mature, older version. But that's where we want to be anyway, right? Who needs youth when you can have wisdom instead? We are going to tap into your strengths and use them to reenergize your life. We will find fun ways to add that sparkle back that you miss when life gets hard. We are going to build on what we know about ourselves, both strong and not so strong, to develop an arsenal for turning hard days into great ones.

It doesn't have to take a lot of time. We are all crazy busy, right? You have my permission to think about these things just when you are alone. Like in the shower or standing outside of the van pumping gas while the kids are still strapped in. Just pay attention. Look around and soak in the goodness God gave you. We are going to tap into what is amazing about you and use it to make your life better and glorify God.

It's easier than you think! Like Dorothy and her red shoes, you have the power already. You just need to realize it.

Your simple assignment:

1. Think of one thing you find easy to do, and soak in the beauty of that quality.

2. Make a mental list of five physical objects you love. (No right or wrong answers here!)

3. Write down your top five best and top five worst qualities.

4. Read Matthew 25:14–30.

CHAPTER 2

What's Your Dream?

> I will instruct you and teach you in the way you
> should go; I will counsel you with my loving eye on
> you. (Psalm 32:8)

I have vivid childhood memories of being in my grandmother's kitchen on Christmas Day. Her kitchen was tiny, but it would bustle with half a dozen ladies, each preparing her assigned portion of the dinner. Grandmother would set me in a corner in front of her orange counter, right next to the phone on the wall, with an empty bowl and a bag of string beans. My job was to snap the beans into the bowl and answer the phone if it rang. "Don't move or you will get in the way," she would whisper to me.

I had no intention of moving. I had the best seat in the house. From where I was, I could see every woman stirring and chatting and slipping their hands into pot holders to check the food in the oven. My grandmother stood on the other side of the counter from me, and while she rolled out piecrusts or peeled potatoes, she would answer questions from the aunts and neighbors who were there to join us for the meal. She was very graceful and seemed to have every detail under control, like a well-choreographed dance. She directed the movements in beautiful harmony, right down to the arrangement of the marshmallows on the sweet potato pie.

Every now and then, she would glance over at me, and our eyes would meet. She would wink at me like we had a special secret. In my imagination, she was imparting to me the wisdom I would later need to prepare this meal on my own, for my future family.

And that became my dream. I longed to be like her and have a whole crowd of family and friends feasting around a table piled high with steaming bowls of mashed potatoes and gravy. I wanted to hear the rave reviews of another year's meal well done. She made it look effortless. And she obviously loved doing it, a passion I didn't understand as I snapped beans and observed.

By the time I had a family of my own, my grandmother had long since passed away. Holiday meals continued with the aunts and neighbors, and we all still loved getting together and using her recipes. Somewhere deep inside of me, I felt she had passed the mantle to me in those glances across the orange counter. In the early too-poor-to-buy-toilet-paper years of my marriage, it was impossible for me to host any large gatherings. Not only did I not have money, but our teeny duplex barely fit the rickety card table we used as a combination dining room/workstation.

When I finally moved into a house that was big enough, and I could actually afford to buy a turkey, I jumped on the chance to realize my dream. I announced that I wanted to host the Christmas meal.

By that time in my life, I had six children under the age of eight. Uh-huh, yep. Obviously I was in some kind of postpartum fog brain to think I could pull off an entire holiday dinner complete with seven kinds of pie and homemade rolls. But I tend to go overboard on things, so nothing was going to stop me.

What I lacked in cooking skills, I planned to mask with gorgeous centerpieces and creative place settings. I arranged flowers and made lists, and I had a chart magneted to the fridge with each step of the meal preparation scheduled down to the minute. And if you're wondering, my grandmother never had a chart. It seemed to be all in her head. But I am a list maker, so that was my victory strategy.

Besides my lifelong training of snapping beans to prepare me, I worked for days beforehand and assigned a few dishes to some of the family and friends who were coming to my feast. But I really wanted to "bless" the people coming by doing most of the work, so I overloaded myself and, frankly, had expectations that were way too high.

But it was my dream, and I was going to shoot for the moon and not let the small fact that I had three toddlers and a newborn stop me from hosting the Best Christmas EVER. Forget that I didn't pencil "nurse the baby" into my schedule and that I assumed my husband was going to follow my agenda and that I had no idea how to cook a turkey. I set my alarm for four thirty in the morning. By nine o'clock, I began to wonder if this was going to work. And when my three-year-old threw up on the middle of the kitchen floor, I saw my Norman Rockwell moment quickly disappearing.

That's how dreams go, isn't it? They never turn out the way we think they will. Sometimes they are better than we could have imagined. Sometimes they are worse. Much worse. Either way, they are almost always a surprise. We must dare to dream anyway and trust that God will do what He wants with it. It is in the act of believing for something bigger than ourselves that we express our uniqueness and inspire others.

I love the book *Restless* by Jennie Allen. She has a wonderful way of describing our uniqueness: "Our creative God has an infinite number of creative plans to make himself known through us, his image bearers, so he sent his Spirit to give unique visions to unique people to reach the world in unique and beautiful ways."[1]

Imagine … God using you and me to reach the world!

I am definitely a dreamer. And combined with my OCD tendencies, I get ideas in my head and I hold on to them like a quarterback holds the ball as he runs for the winning touchdown (there's your sports analogy for the entire book). Like everyone, I have big dreams and small dreams and middle-sized dreams and a few that are the size of the galaxy. Or at least they feel like it to me.

Our dreams are one way we can understand our individuality and learn to embrace the uniqueness God gave us. In order to make the most of our time here on earth, we have to understand what it is He is asking of us. He gives us His Word as a rich source of wisdom and instruction, but in many areas we also need a way to know what it is that we, as individuals, are supposed to do. There is clear direction for how to treat our neighbor, but not so much on topics such as employment or how many pairs of shoes one needs.

> In their hearts humans plan their course, but the
> LORD establishes their steps. (Prov. 16:9)

A DREAM IS A WISH YOUR HEART MAKES ...

Through our hopes and dreams we develop an understanding of what success and adventure mean to us. That definition is different for everyone because we are supposed to be different. Even the most alike people have wildly contrasting ideas of what they want their lives to look like.

Some dreams have been a part of us since childhood. We dreamed of becoming something when we grew up ... maybe you wanted to be a ballerina or a movie star. One of my fantasies was to be an actress and I was pretty sure, if I put my mind to it, I could take Broadway by storm. As I am sure you have figured out, that never happened. I did play Kanga in a local theater production of *Winnie-the-Pooh*, but I really think I got the part because I was so "motherly and bouncy."

When you are a child, people often ask, "What do you want to be when you grow up?" When people asked me that question I would always reply, "I want to be a mother, a teacher, and an interior designer." (Winning Tony Awards was more of a secret dream that I kept to myself.) I never really purposely put myself on the path to any of those things, but it was still my dream. I just had no idea how to really make it happen.

Some of that, the acting dream for example, was really more of a fantasy than something I really thought might happen. But I did think I could do the others ... motherhood, teaching, and interior design. I had a knack for those things from the beginning of my life. And frankly, even though I wasn't going to become an actress, I was pretty good at drama too ... just not the kind that takes place on the stage.

The occupational dreams of children tell us a lot about what their natural calling is. I clearly wasn't called to be a theater star, but if I look deeper into that desire, I can see how I organically worked that into my life. I speak at conferences, I frequently act out history stories in our homeschool, and I dramatically read aloud to the kids and bring the books to life—all skills needed to be an actress. Just with a *much* smaller audience. And younger. And less critical.

When you were a child and someone asked you what you wanted to be, what did you say? While I was steady with my reply to that question, my best girlfriend had a different answer for each day of the year. One day she was planning to become a veterinarian and the next day she would declare that she would go to beauty school. If you are like her with a long list of childhood dreams, that's fine! You are unique and wonderful, and your changing dreams are part of what makes you fascinating.

In the same way that we identified some of your gifts and talents, let's also dig around in your head and figure out what your dreams are.

No matter how many dreams you had as a child, you can do this quick exercise. Think of three of your childhood dreams. That's it. Easy, right? Even though you may not be able to fully realize those dreams anymore, let's look into the heart of your dreams and see what we can pull out that will help you learn to reset and improve your life.

You have buried passions and secret visions that should be playing a part in your life now. It's important to know what ignites your fire so that you can make the most of all of your resources. In *Restless* Allen also said, "We want to live our lives intentionally. Without some effort, we will waste our minutes, our days … our lives. So putting thought into intentionally spending our time and resources for the glory of God may be the most important thing we do with our lives."[2]

It sounds weird, but I didn't really know how to become an interior designer, which made me think it wasn't really an option. However, I never lost that passion and I used it in my life despite not getting any formal education for design. I dared to let myself enjoy decorating my own home with ideas that popped into my head that I had never seen anywhere else. For instance, I have an old refrigerator in my living room that we use as a cabinet for blankets. And I painted my piano aqua, despite the protests of everyone I told. I paid attention to what I liked in a beautiful room, either in a magazine or someone's house, and I taught myself some simple design skills from that. Eventually, I began to share my own home on my blog and was noticed by several magazines and other designers who invited me to work with them.

So, while I never became a "real" interior designer, I do feel like that dream came true for me, and God has used it in ways that I wouldn't have understood as a child (for one thing the Internet didn't exist then). The same is true for my dream of being a teacher. I didn't take the usual route to that, but I homeschool my own children, so I definitely tapped into those natural instincts. And you know what happened to that dream of becoming a mother. Who would have ever thought God would give me that times NINE?

If you dreamed of, say, being a soccer player, but never did it, I'll bet there's a way you are using that interest now. If not, then ask yourself, why not? Is there something you could do to develop that in yourself? Could you coach a children's soccer team? Could you teach your own kids a few tricks that you picked up in your younger years? Or maybe you could write a blog or start a social media support for soccer enthusiasts.

Just because the winds of life forced you away from those childhood dreams doesn't mean they aren't important! You had those visions for a reason.

YOU KNOW YOU'RE A GROWN-UP WHEN ...

In adulthood there are other kinds of dreams, the ones you don't think much about as a child. Being debt free is a great example of this. Few of us grow up thinking, *I want to be a ballerina and have no credit card debt*. The idea that money would be such a huge part of our lives is a distant concept when we are young. But then we get married and have some struggles and a few kids and all of a sudden dreaming can become more of a nightmare. The pressure of financial burdens can affect anyone's hope. Debt is a dream killer. But, like anything else, it can be turned around! We can reset anything with some determination and patience.

Most of us are familiar with the teachings of Dave Ramsey. We follow his wisdom, like this quote from his book *Total Money Makeover*: "My financial life began turning around when I took responsibility for it,"[3] and that helps us turn the dream-killing debt around. It is time we take responsibility for not only our finances but all of our dreams of a richer life!

And what about a happy marriage? It never occurs to us that the guy who makes our heart melt when we say "I do" will break our hearts so many times along the road of life. For many of us, a happy marriage seems like a distant possibility and we lose hope for the future. The same goes for health, friendships, motivation, or your children's well-being/spiritual life.

Grown-up dreams are a vital part of life. Dreaming of great health doesn't make you a fossil; it makes you wise.

EVERYDAY DREAMER

And then there are the smallest dreams of all … the ones that are a part of daily life. I wake up each morning with a heart full of possibilities for the day ahead. Then it all comes crashing down around me before I make it to the kitchen to fix breakfast (here in Texas, we "fix" food).

Do you dream of an uninterrupted shower? A meal that consists of more than your kids' leftover sandwich crust smeared with peanut butter? Do you wish you could ever have a place to wear that cute new sweater you got for Christmas? Do you dream of having a friendship like Oprah and Gayle?

These are normal everyday dreams, and so often they seem like they can never come true. To make it worse, you see everyone on Instagram having coffee with her girlfriend, wearing cute boots, and looking *so* happy. Ugh.

It's those perfect-looking social media images that send me into my whiny, pouty place. I mean, it's one thing to lose hope of ever being in a Broadway musical (Oh yes, didn't I tell you? It *had* to be a musical), but to lose the teeniest hope of being clean, fed, and friended while everyone else practically has rainbows arched over her head can put me in a lifelong bad mood.

When the kids were all really young, there were days when I would be in tears by the time my husband got home from work. I would beg him, BEG HIM, to watch the kids so I could take a shower by myself. And as much as he sympathized, it never really happened. He tried. But one of the kids would escape from him just long enough to find me. Just as I was letting the hot streams of relaxing goodness pelt down my back, I would hear "Mommy, I NEED you!" seconds before one of them ripped the shower curtain back and jumped in the shower with me. Fully clothed. Holding my cell phone.

The life we pictured for ourselves can seem so far away when we are in the throes of mothering toddlers or driving older kids from one guitar lesson to the next karate class without having time to stop to go to the bathroom. When you are this close to considering wearing Depends for the sake of convenience, you need a do-over.

#WINNING #ALLTHEDREAMS

They're all connected ... our big dreams and small dreams. If we are defeated and hopeless in one area, that defeat and hopelessness spills over into other areas of our lives. It doesn't really matter how big the defeat is. We lose hope, and hopelessness spreads. We stop trying, and our belief that we can succeed at anything is undermined. Is there a way you can put yourself on the path of your dreams? Those dreams are not just for you ... they are for everyone! God wants us all to be seeking a life of goodness and joy. Financial freedom and happy marriages definitely fall into that category. So many of us have fallen into traps of debt and misery that we don't know how to get ourselves out. The prospect of it taking years of energy and stress to get ourselves back on track feels overwhelming. But it *is* possible, and I want you to know that you are able to not only build a healthier lifestyle but also have joy through the midst of the changes.

Here's a little more truth from Dave, in his book *Financial Peace Revisited*: "To think that the handling of your personal finances is merely a matter of math control is naive. You must get better control of all aspects of your life. Until you do, [even the best advice] will have little effect but will instead be neutralized by the other habits in your life."[4]

Do you want to try? Do you want to "reset" and believe that you can? Have you truly identified what it is that you want? It is good to work to achieve the things God has placed in your heart and to push against any obstacles in your life. It's even better to look to God for direction in those difficult areas.

> The LORD will guide you always; he will satisfy your
> needs in a sun-scorched land and will strengthen
> your frame. You will be like a well-watered garden,
> like a spring whose waters never fail. (Isa. 58:11)

BUT HOW?

At the end of this chapter, I'm going to give you a simple assignment based on what we have covered here. Be sure to remember that all dreams matter—big, medium, and small. (Remember Goldilocks? The small bed was just right for her. It isn't always the big stuff that makes a difference.) All dreams are important. Those small, seemingly insignificant wishes are the glue that holds our days together. Turning one of those small struggles around has the potential to be the first domino in a long line of issues you need to knock down.

As we look at what we want, we shouldn't put any stock in wishing for a life of ease. God wants us to follow a path that will lead us to the kind of true dreams that will fulfill us in a way nothing else can. If your dream is for an easy, problem-free life, then you need to work on adjusting that idea. There is never going to be an easy life, although here in America we have it pretty great. If you wake up each morning wishing all of your struggles would disappear, you will be disappointed, just the same as if you woke up wishing to have the perfect body or be twenty years younger. It is an impossible dream and one you need to let go of in order to find true joy.

But if you wake up every morning and simply hope that you can actually drink your coffee while it's hot or be able to find your shoes without tearing the house apart, those are reasonable ideals. These are problems that, with some creativity and determination, you can eliminate. Or at least lessen. God is always there to direct you to the reset that you need to turn those struggles around.

We must always start with seeking Him through investing time in prayer and Bible reading. This is the beginning of really grabbing hold of the goals He has for us. The depth of satisfaction that the joy of the Holy Spirit brings us cannot be compared to a childhood occupational dream coming true.

I am beautifully reminded through these verses that His Word is the first place to start when I am trying to make changes in my life:

I will be fully satisfied as with the richest of foods;
with singing lips my mouth will praise you. On my
bed I remember you; I think of you through the
watches of the night. Because you are my help, I
sing in the shadow of your wings. (Ps. 63:5–7)

The shadow of His wings is where we can find joy! Wow. I want to be there.

Let's take a hard look and figure out what derailed you from the dreams that seemed possible for you so many years ago. How did you get so far away from that girl who thought she could take on the world and win?

The first step to not getting depressed over our lack of accomplishing our dreams is to realize that most of those childhood dreams were simply a world of possibility that we didn't understand. We had no way to know where our talents would take us, so we grabbed on to activities that looked like they would satisfy our cravings. As much as I wanted to be an interior designer, I would have been terrible at running an office and keeping appointments and filing receipts. Children sometimes dream what they can see and have no idea that there are many, many other ways to quench the thirst they feel. God knows your innermost secrets, and if you give Him those dreams, He will direct your path in a way that will satisfy you even more than accomplishing those childhood fantasies.

Second, just because you didn't accomplish all your dreams does *not* mean you are a failure! If we set before ourselves a path that is too narrow, then we have nowhere to go when life changes direction. Things happen that interrupt what we want. Sometimes we cause them ourselves, and sometimes they happen to us. Either way, they can alter what is available to us. But it isn't a failure. It is a new possibility.

Bethany Hamilton dreamed of becoming a world champion surfer. She practiced and sacrificed and built her skills. Then one sunny day while she was paddling the waves, she was attacked by a shark, and her left arm was bitten completely off. In the aftermath of the attack and the loss of her arm, she knew she had to adjust her dream or lose all hope. She slowly built a new set of skills, and now that time and experience have passed, she sees all of the changes as a beautiful opportunity. In her book *Soul Surfer* she wrote, "You make your own adventure in life. And I truly believe that if you open your eyes to your surroundings, there's lots of neat stuff to be found practically anywhere on earth."[5] Her new dream is that her story will inspire others to pick up their Bibles.

She had the opportunity to reset in a huge way. But what you have to overcome is no less important. You may not have a movie made about you, but you are doing the work God has set for you, and your soul satisfaction waits right there for you. Where your hidden dreams feel lost, God is waiting to find a better you than you could have imagined.

Your dreams are still there. They may be buried way down below a pile of bills, and you may be feeling so tired and overwhelmed that you can't even think. But they are there, and we can resurrect them. That girl who was really good at working with animals when she was young but who got pregnant and has spent the past ten years just trying to survive is still gifted with animals! There is a way she can build a new dream to include her gifts and talents.

She may have to let go of becoming a veterinarian, but she can still find her way back to that passion. She could volunteer at a shelter, help her neighbors with their pets, or teach children how to care for animals.

Jennie Allen, in *Restless*, shares, "Don't dream of winning Super Bowls or even Saturday's game on Monday morning. Win practice that day, in that moment. Win that day, whatever it holds."[6]

Sometimes our dreams can be a cry for help. I have been through times when my biggest dream was simply to enjoy my life again. I felt like I was nothing but a constant drip of "No" and "Stop that!" for my family. I wanted to be fun, but it got all sapped out of me with childbirth recovery and eating strained peas for lunch because I was too tired to find food for myself. We can feel like we are wasting our lives and like we'll never feel satisfied. We all go through that at some point, *all* of us. Thankfully there is a way out from that depth of a lack of joy through faith and trust. God waits to lead you back to the cool, still waters of delighting in what lies ahead.

HOPE IS ON THE WAY!

Don't lose hope. You are in the midst of an opportunity to see your life in a new way. Those dreams of your past can meet with your present and influence the future. You are still you, even though it can be hard to see sometimes.

Life can sure seem to derail even the simplest of dreams. And not just the big interruptions, like having kids or losing a job, but also small issues, like getting the flu or the babysitter canceling, can take your train from full steam ahead to a full stop in seconds.

What prevents you from becoming who you dreamed of all those years ago? So often we discover we don't really have the talent to live out what we thought we wanted. Or we compare ourselves to others in the field and find ourselves falling short of that standard. Our own thoughts of feeling unworthy or unwanted can stop us from going far with our passions.

We let insecurity and lack of easy opportunity tell us that we can't have our dreams. But it's not true! You have a gift, and your dreams should be tapping into it. You will have to let go of your idea of what the ideal looks like and grab hold of something even better—God's will for the fulfillment of your life.

And the smallest dreams of all, a simple shower or trip to the potty without people screaming on the other side of the door, are within your reach. They may not turn out exactly the way you think they should. But they are there. God gives us all of the tools we need to reach the dream we have of a nice day with our kids and husband. We already have patience, gentleness, and self-control. We just need to learn to use them.

A CHRISTMAS TO REMEMBER

The day my family arrived for my first ever Christmas at my house was not quite the glowing success I had hoped for. The turkey had a weird taste, the rolls wouldn't rise, and I never did figure out how to get all of the food to the table while still hot. Think cold mashed potatoes ... yuck. My table settings were very pretty though. Even before Pinterest was available for inspiration, I would go out and cut vines and branches and wrap them in burlap to make centerpieces.

Little did I know that one of the vines I cut that morning was poison ivy. For the next three weeks I had painful rashes on my arms from those beautiful table decorations.

As I watched my dream Christmas go down in flames, I did a do-over. I couldn't make a gourmet meal, but I knew that one thing I could do well was create memories. While people were clearing their places, I quickly wrote out little discussion cards and spread them all around the tables. They were intended to stir up conversations with questions like, "Who would you invite to dinner if you could ask anyone in history?" or "What was your favorite class in school?" Being a competitive bunch, we turned it into a game and started pelting each other with these questions. Someone kept score (I don't even remember how we came up with the rules), and we all had a blast. It turned out that while I wasn't as good as my grandmother at producing a fabulous meal, I did have her ability to make strangers feel welcome and comfortable (an attribute of being an interior designer that I never thought of before that day).

I continued to host the holiday meal every year after that, and I got better at making rolls, but it is still a mystery to me how people get all the food to the table while it's hot. I don't have a minute-by-minute plan hanging on the fridge anymore. I don't need it since I buy most of the food already cooked (I'm no dummy) and ask the guests to make more of a contribution than I used to. Now it has become more of a party than just a meal, and we invite as many friends as we can possibly squeeze into our little farmhouse. My kitchen just about bursts with people and goodies and dirty dishes and laughter. I know now that this is the dream my grandmother was passing on to me. It was about hosting a holiday meal that people would remember with fondness because they felt loved in my home.

And as an added bonus, I eventually learned to decorate without using poisonous plants.

Your simple assignment:

1. Write down three dreams you had as a child.

2. Write down three dreams you have now as an adult.

3. Think of three ways those dreams are all connected. (This is to see the connection between you then and you now!)

4. Read Psalm 139:13–16.

CHAPTER 3

What Is Your Problem?

The Serenity Prayer

God, grant me the serenity to accept
the things I cannot change,
The courage to change the things I can,
And the wisdom to know the difference.

My three-year-old daughter had been leaning over the dining room table for half an hour, coloring a picture. I could see with my peripheral vision that her face was scrunched up with lines of deep concentration. When she finished she grabbed the paper, bounced over, and presented it to me. "It's YOU, Mommy!" She beamed as she laid her masterpiece in my hand. I looked down to see a child-like drawing of a smiling woman standing next to a table where her family sat, and she was holding a loaf of bread. Not your normal, light-brown, can't-wait-to-dig-into-it looking bread. This loaf was black, and there was a huge billow of smoke rising from it.

She really didn't have to tell me that the woman holding a charred brick and serving it to her family was supposed to be me.

I recognized myself.

People say that the kitchen is the heart of the home. If that is true then my home's heart represents burned cookies and whatever recently spilled over on the stove. While God generously bestows gifts upon us all, cooking is not one He gave to me.

I have always admired people who can really cook. It would be so lovely to present my family with gourmet dinners that would make the Barefoot Contessa proud. (I mention her because people say she is my twin!) I can close my eyes and picture a gorgeous presentation of rack of lamb with roasted vegetables in the center of my flea-market made-over table. In my imagination there is the aroma of garlic and fresh herbs wafting through the house. People's mouths are watering with anticipation. But that has never happened in the twenty-eight years James and I have been married. Because when my eyes are actually open, I can't even get a hard-boiled egg to come out right. There are about four dishes I can turn out pretty well, so we just stick to those and vary them by adding cheese or bacon.

Looking at my problem of constantly burning food, I know that some of it is lack of talent, but most of it is lack of focus. I don't burn bread because I am unable to pull the loaf from the oven at the right time. I burn bread because I tell myself I can go do something else for the twenty-five minutes it's baking, and then I get lost in another project and forget the bread. Until I hear the smoke alarm going off, a sound my children are all too familiar with.

I sometimes wonder if they would even scramble for a real fire. It's more likely they would hear the alarm and think to themselves, *Dinner's ready.*

So many times we think our problems come from something outside of ourselves. We can't get the bank account balanced because our spouse doesn't write down all the withdrawals. We don't finish the Sunday school preparations because the kids won't stay in bed while we try to work on it late at night. Our pants don't fit because the only food we could find to eat yesterday was a pan of brownies and a half-empty bag of Tostitos.

But the truth is that most of our problems stem from something more inside of us than we want to admit. When I am baking bread, I could stay in the kitchen and pay attention to the oven. I could find something to fill the time that keeps me in the same room, or I could learn to let other projects go so I am not feeling so pulled in a dozen different directions.

It takes a special kind of strength to admit that we are our own biggest problem. I say that in victory, not as a victim. It is a victory to see that I could take control over how I spend those twenty-five baking minutes and stop blaming the oven. It is victim mentality when I tell myself I am just too scatterbrained to ever bake a decent loaf of bread.

WHAT'S YOUR LABEL?

I once knew a woman who believed her problem of excessive worrying was out of her control. She hovered over her kids and tried to control her friends and masked it by saying how worried she was, as if it was genuine concern instead of manipulation. She could frequently be heard saying, "I can't help it. I am a worrier." Her faith was more in her own "nature" than in what God says in His Word. He promises to meet our every need and give us comfort. He urges us to trust Him and not worry:

> Do not be anxious about anything, but in every situation, by prayer and petition, with thanksgiving, present your requests to God. And the peace of God, which transcends all understanding, will guard your hearts and your minds in Christ Jesus. (Phil. 4:6–7)

If you call yourself a worrier or a control freak or a screamer, you are condemning yourself to a stale life. It may be extra hard for you to move past the reactions you have, but it is possible. The more work it takes for you to overcome, the better your testimony will be! If you will see beyond what you think of as an impossible-to-change trait, you will see a radically different picture of yourself. You will see hope and trust and peace that passes understanding. You will see a woman who inspires others with her joy for life and love of God.

Do you want that? You are not a worrier; you are a woman who struggles with worry and is ready to give all of that over to a God who promises to lead you to a life rich with blessings! You are not a screamer; you are someone who has gotten into a habit of over-reacting, and there is a place of hope for you where you will be able to stop doing that.

I love the book *Unglued* by Lysa TerKeurst. She addresses this issue often through the book, and here is one of my favorite quotes:

> Labels are awful. They imprison us in categories that are hard to escape. I should know. While I've

never been a numbered inmate in a federal prison,
I've put labels on myself that have certainly locked
me into hard places.[1]

As we explore our problems, no matter what they are, it is best to start within ourselves and work our way outward. But instead we generally do the opposite. First I see how everyone or everything else caused my problem and then I might look at the possibility that there is the teeniest thing I could have contributed.

What problem drew you to this book? Do your kids drive you nuts? Are you overwhelmed with responsibilities? There is a way to get through that with joy and hope and confidence. We aren't going to take away our problems. We are shooting to take away our negative response to the problems.

I want to help you pick those hard days apart and find out what the problem really is. Is there a way to make your situation more manageable by altering something you are doing? Do you have control over any part of it? Very rarely are we 100 percent at the mercy of outside circumstances.

We really only see a true helpless situation in the movies: the asteroids are raining down, and the townspeople are literally running for their lives. The world is lost until Bruce Willis steps in and heroically saves everyone. Without him, the world as we know it would no longer exist. If this actually happens to you, you have my permission to blame outside circumstances for all your problems. Including your belly fat and overdrawn bank account.

But for those of us not in a movie, we probably have time during a trial to stop for a minute and evaluate. We can breathe, look around, and take mental notes. Rarely are we ever in a life-or-death crisis, even though it feels like it much of the time. There are always areas of the problem that we can point to as something we could have done better, and we can learn from those. It's not just about taking responsibility; it's taking charge of what you can change.

Consider this: if all your circumstances are the cause of your problems, then you have no way to change them. But if you had a part in creating the problem, then you can find a way to get over it. Jump that hurdle, friends!

One issue that touches most of our lives is feeling like we don't have enough time. In the case of the previously mentioned unfinished Sunday school lessons, it may not be completely the kids' fault. If I take an honest look at how I spent my time for the past week, there are gaps. The night I watched three back-to-back episodes of *The Biggest Loser* could have been better spent working for an hour on my Sunday school lessons instead. Then, afterward, I could have let myself unwind by watching only one episode of my show. Or, if I could multitask, I could have done them at the same time: cut a few construction-paper Jesus figures, cheer on my favorite contestant, glue glitter on an angel, cry over a makeover, and so on.

Time is the great equalizer. We all have the same amount of hours in a day, and what we choose to do with those hours is up to us. It may feel like it's out of our control, but if we are willing to see it, the truth is that we are choosing. I chose the commitments I made; I chose to homeschool; I chose to repaint the kitchen; I chose to help a friend; and so on. What are you choosing that is taking up your time?

THE VICTIM OR THE VICTOR

Then there are kid problems. Talk to any mom … we *all* have them. Don't let someone's happy pictures on social media convince you that her mornings are mocha latte cappuccinos while you're drowning in cold, spilled instant coffee. Everyone has messes. Everyone needs to find a better way through her struggles. I can't say that enough because our minds convince us otherwise. We believe the magazine-worthy photos of other people's homes as if they live that way all the time. It is not true.

One reason I know for sure that we all deal with kid issues is because kids constantly change. That makes it impossible to ever get rid of the problems we have to deal with. Just when you feel like you finally have a grip on getting them to stay in their beds at night, they start something new. They begin to hate school, and now you have to go back to the drawing board and try to figure out how to deal with this new thing. Friends, they are supposed to do that! They are growing and maturing. It's a good thing!

But that doesn't make it any easier. It can wear you plumb out.

The good news is that while your kids are coming up with new ways to challenge you every day, you have a constant source of help and inspiration. God does His part. He has answers for you and does unseen miracles daily on your behalf. But you have to do your part in accepting that you have the strength, tools, and wisdom to not only get through your issues but also become better because of them.

Often, we get upset and irritated instead. We get angry that our son has forgotten to take out the trash. Again. So instead of turning to the truth, which is that we play a part in this situation, we become the victim. Friends, you are not victim to the issues your kids have. Believe me, I know it feels that way. But you are absolutely in charge of your own responses and reactions. I'll tell you what I mean.

I often set my expectations way too high. So when one child pretends to forget to wash the dishes and another loses his school-work and a third child won't come out of the bathroom, it throws me into a tizzy. Have you ever been in a tizzy? I can live there if I am not careful.

Things get in my way, and I fall apart. We allow unexpected circumstances to throw a wrench in our plans, and we don't see the truth—that we are within easy reach of joy and accomplishment.

My children do not cause my tizzies. They may act badly, and they definitely have areas they need to work on—and we will do that together. But for me to get angry, frustrated, and lose control is my own doing.

When I see the trash can overflowing while my son lounges on the couch playing games on his iPod, I get almost instantly incensed. My mental conversation begins, "WHY doesn't he CARE about this? Now I have to stop my life and deal with his refusal to do this simple job …" And on and on I go. By the time I am reminding him to put down his game and take out the trash, I am angry and it comes out in my tone. That either puts him on the defensive or makes him feel defeated and unloved. That is not my goal at all. I just want the trash taken out.

Instead, take a step back and breathe in a long, slow breath and a prayer. Ask God to intervene with wisdom in how to manage this problem. At the very least, let His love for you and your son wash over you. Let Him show you how small this is and that your goal is to love your son, not turn him against you.

There have been many, many times when I prayed this prayer and God gave me a crazy, creative idea for how to handle the problem. In this case, God showed me that the task was not obvious to my son. I had been expecting him to know what I wanted, when what he actually needed was a more specific job. So instead of "take out the trash when it's full," the job became "check the trash can every morning before breakfast and each night after dinner." If it gets full in between, then it's not automatically his job. That helped a lot, but he still didn't always manage it, so I added a consequence. If he doesn't do his clearly defined job, then he has to go around to every person in the house while holding a trash bag and ask if there is any trash he can take out for them (if you can't think of a creative consequence for your child, acts of service are always a good fallback!). Like any teenager, he still doesn't do it all the time, and we still struggle with it every once in a while, but not very often. When he messes up I don't lose my cool about it, because I know there are new solutions if I need them. And I don't want to make the problem worse by convincing him that because of a can of garbage he has less value to me.

There will always be interruptions and obstacles to accomplishing our dreams. You know what? They are blessings! If life was a steady flow of unobstructed pathways, how would we ever learn or grow or understand the depth of the beauty that surrounds us? There is great value in having to learn to jump a hurdle or move a huge block out of the way.

In her amazing book *Cold Tangerines*, Shauna Niequist says it this way:

When you can invest yourself deeply and unremittingly in the life that surrounds you instead of declaring yourself out of the game once and for all, because what's happened to you is too bad, too deep, too ugly for anyone to expect you to move on from, that's that good, rich place. That's the place where the things that looked for all intents and purposes like curses start to stand up and shimmer and dance, and you realize with a gasp that they may have been blessings all along.[2]

Hard days happen to all of us. I really should make that into a bumper sticker. (One thing you need to know about me is that I dream up useless and pointless business ideas twenty-four hours a day … seriously. I wake up and write them down, like this bumper sticker brilliance.) No one, not the richest man in the world, is without his share of really hard days. In fact, the Bible says it will be easier to go through the eye of a needle than for that rich guy to get into heaven. Think on that! If you don't like how hard it is to get your daughter to eat her veggies without a battle, what would it be like to have to squeeze through the eye of a needle?! I mean, ouch!

DEALING WITH THE LAUNDRY MOUNTAIN

Let's put one of your problems under the microscope and find the parts you can work with to turn it around.

Something we all deal with is laundry {cue dreadful music}. Many of us just can't get our laundry done. As simple as it seems it should be, this can be a problem! Even for those of us who have washing machines right in our home, finding time and space and energy to concentrate on washing, drying, sometimes even ironing (yes, I said the "I" word), folding, and putting clean clothes away can be a real challenge.

What happens is you get really busy, you put it off, and you get a bigger and bigger pile of dirty clothes until you are facing the Mount Everest of all laundry piles. Before you know it, you are staring down the barrel of an entire week of doing nothing but laundry just to catch up. You're now considering pushing the wheelbarrow into the house, loading it up, and hauling all the dirty clothes to the backyard for a bonfire.

Trust me, I understand this predicament. Having nine kids and living on a farm (which, if you don't know, creates a lot more laundry than the normal suburban family lifestyle) is a laundry nightmare. There was a time when I could not keep up with laundry no matter what I tried. I developed several systems that each ultimately fell apart. The worst idea I had was one that had me smelling the kids' clothes each night to decide what needed to be washed and what could go back in the drawer. I know. Not the best. But I was desperate.

So what is the real problem here? Is it that I've got too many kids, and they don't take care of their things, and my husband doesn't help enough, and I need an extra machine? And anything else that will prove this isn't my fault? Or if I take the problem apart bit by bit and am truly honest with myself, can I see that I play a big role in making it more difficult? Yes, the reasons I listed are all valid and need a little bit of exploring, but maybe I could make a difference on my own.

Ask yourself, "If none of the circumstances change, is there a way I can solve this problem anyway?"

If I look closely, I would notice that I go in and out of the laundry room all day and don't always stop to take care of the load that needs attention. I could make that a habit. I could also make a rule for myself not to push the clean clothes off the sofa but to fold them instead. I could teach the kids to do a better job of putting away their own clothes and follow through by checking. I could set aside just ten minutes each afternoon after naptime to fold a few things. In fact, if I really looked at it, I could fix almost this entire problem with small changes in my own actions.

I did eventually get a pretty good handle on my laundry issues by doing those things. And what I discovered is that it wasn't even that difficult. I made a personal rule that every time I walk through the laundry room I check to see if there's anything that needs to be moved around—a load ready to toss in the washer or moved into the dryer or emptied from the dryer and carried to the folding area. Now that my kids are older, I have asked them to do the same. I made "fold laundry" an afternoon chore for several of the younger kids, and every night before they go to bed I make sure they have put it all in its proper place. It's not perfect, but we don't struggle with laundry mountains anymore.

And guess what? I still have too many kids, and they don't always take care of their things, and my husband has never, to my recollection, helped with the laundry. And yet I solved the problem. And I'm not exhausted from the process.

There is always something you can do to make a difficult situation better, even if it is a simple attitude change. Yes, I said it. Our own attitudes have everything to do with getting that do-over we so desperately need. So hang on to your hats, because we are about to go there.

Philippians 1:6 says, "[I am] confident of this, that he who began a good work in you will carry it on to completion until the day of Christ Jesus." God uses this verse to tell me I *can* trust Him to show me what I need to become the woman He started so long ago when I was a baby. He knew those laundry piles would be in my future, and He prepared me for them.

Now it's time for *me* to see my problems for what they truly are: something God can use to complete the good work He started in me!

I DON'T LIKE YOUR ATTITUDE RIGHT NOW

How many times a day do you tell your kids, "You need to change your attitude about that," and expect them to listen? Yet when God says to us, "My child, you need to trust Me and let Me take care of this," we kick and stomp and fight Him every step of the way. *That's NOT FAIR!* I scream in my head. I may look like a fully formed adult on the outside, but I am often a whining baby-child on the inside.

I don't like to be corrected for my attitude, because I think I have a right to it. If I adjust my mind-set I am in danger of not getting my way, and we cannot have that. No sirree.

The thing is, if we are not willing to acknowledge that our attitude is the biggest reason we have most of our problems, we will stay stuck on the carousel of struggle. Around and around and around … never really getting anywhere. The ups and downs fool us into believing that our problems are getting better or worse, but it's an illusion.

We first need to explore our expectations. Meal preparation, for example, is an area I go into with preconceived ideas that I am not even aware of. Most of these expectations are reasonable. I assume I should be able to find the knife I need for cutting potatoes, and the milk should not have gone bad in the fridge before the expiration date. Then, when the knife is nowhere to be found and the milk smells sour, I start to lose my cool. I fuss and blame others and let myself believe I wasn't given what I need to achieve success.

The lost knife and the spoiled milk interrupt my groove, and to top it off, I have a limited amount of time to get this job done. People are hungry around here! If you asked me right that moment what my problem was I would make a list of irritations that, in my mind, make my life hard. But if I stop and see it through a God's-eye view, the picture is very different.

He sees a frantic woman digging through drawers and the dishwasher in search of a knife. He sees anger as she dumps the milk down the sink while mumbling curses under her breath. Her heart has turned away from joy and embraced her right to an easy time of meal preparation.

My problem may look like milk and knives on the outside, but the truth is that my problem is me. My tendency is to keep such a tight grip on my plans that they can't be wrangled from my hand no matter how hard the pull. I am going to make that planned meal if I have to call my husband away from work to buy milk and a new knife.

Or, if I manage to pull myself together enough to alter my plans, I continue to grumble, and when my poor husband comes home he gets an earful about how hard my life is.

Here's how it could have looked instead. I can't find the knife and discover I don't have milk. Okay. Change of plans. Pray. I can still use some of the ingredients and maybe pull out that weird chopper thing I got as a gift three Christmases ago and never used. I will use that to cut up the potatoes. If I can't make the sauce I wanted, I can just serve the chicken without it. Yes, it will be dry (honestly, when I cook, it's dry with or without sauce), but that's okay. This will possibly throw me off schedule, but it's what I have to work with. I'll try again tomorrow to have dinner ready on time, and if I keep finding myself running late I will make a renewed effort to either change the time we eat or change what I do in the afternoon.

My attitude can continue to be grateful, happy, productive, and pleasant. I don't need to explain the upset to my husband, or if I do, I can tell it as a funny story of overcoming problems and finding success. We have *so* much more control over our problems than we think we do.

Of course, many problems are more complicated than laundry piles and spoiled milk. Often we struggle with broken relationships or serious health issues or addictions. These types of problems are the same in God's eyes as the lost knife. He knew it would happen to you, He prepared you for it, and He makes a way for you to have joy despite how hard things get.

> But ask the animals, and they will teach you, or the
> birds in the sky, and they will tell you; or speak to

the earth, and it will teach you, or let the fish in the
sea inform you. Which of all these does not know
that the hand of the LORD has done this? In his
hand is the life of every creature and the breath of
all mankind. (Job 12:7–10)

When other people are a piece of your problem, there will be parts
of it you have no control over. You can show kindness and gratitude
all day long, but if the other person has the opposite attitude, you
won't be able to make your problem go away completely. Believe it
or not, you still can have personal victory over it! Even if it's only on
your side. You can't, and shouldn't, try to control your husband or
your friends or other adults.

BAKING BREAD

In my marriage, we are opposites. He loves a tight budget; I love
shopping. He wants steak; I want vegetables. He thinks his jokes are
funny … you get my point.

That can really put a damper on my plans. If I think the boys
need new shoes and he says it's not in the budget, I have a problem. I
can point out to him that their little feet are squished in their shoes,
and they look messy at church, and there is a great sale right now
at the local shoe store. Then he can point out that we are barely
squeaking by, and the mortgage is due next week, and the boys are
fine for the moment with the shoes they have, and maybe in two
weeks we can try to get shoes. My goal … his goal. I tend to get
irritated and want him to make both happen—mortgage *and* shoes

for the boys. So what is my problem here? Is it that I have a stubborn husband? Or that I have a stubborn heart?

Sure, we can probably find a compromise (which usually involves me waiting—ugh, I hate waiting), and we can work something out. My husband definitely cares about my dreams and wants to let me move forward with my ideas, just in a responsible way. The real problem is that I get all in a wad about not getting what I want, and I make the whole thing worse. I get mad or fussy and make us both miserable. If I would simply let him know that I am hoping to do it soon, thank him for trying to work it into the budget, and then just drop it, half of my problems would disappear. I need a magic wand made of wisdom and maturity (new business idea … a maturity stick I could wave around my head when I am acting like a baby-child).

As we move forward to the next chapters, keep in mind what we have learned together: knowing yourself, building your dream, and understanding the problem. We have to be ready to face, head-on, the truth that with a better attitude we have already won half the battle.

Elisabeth Elliot (if you haven't read her personal story, you must), in her sweet book *Keep a Quiet Heart*, shares this beautiful thought:

> In Jesus' last discourse with His disciples before He was crucified (a discourse meant for us as well as for them), He explained that God is the gardener, He Himself is the vine, and we are branches. If we are bearing fruit, then we must be pruned. This is a

painful process. Jesus knew that His disciples would face much suffering. He showed them, in this beautiful metaphor, that it was not for nothing. Only the well-pruned vine bears the best fruit.[3]

I want to be pruned. I want to bear the best fruit.

THE BEAUTY OF A HELPFUL FRIEND

After I saw the drawing of myself with the smoking loaf of bread, I determined to improve my cooking skills, at least enough for the food to be the proper color in my children's artwork. So I asked a friend to come over to help me learn to bake bread. I had been trying it on my own for several years without much success (you can't say I give up easily). This friend is one of those people who have a Midas touch in the kitchen. People beg, BEG, for her to bake them bread, because it's like eating a little slice of heaven in every bite. And, oh, the texture … I am seriously drooling right now as I think about it.

So I asked for her help and she very kindly came. And even better, she brought with her one of her teenage daughters to watch my kids so we could fully focus on the task of baking. Now, *that* is a friend who understands your deepest need.

After a couple of hours I had, rising in my oven, five of the most beautiful loaves of bread you ever saw. She lovingly guided me through each step—measuring, testing the water temperature, kneading, rising, shaping the loaf. I wanted her to stay forever. She would hold up a kitchen tool and ask me if I knew how to use it. If not, she would explain it to me. I know she was purposely identifying my problems and then helping me through them, but it just felt like we were having a lovely day together.

Once the loaves were safely in the oven, she wiped off my counters, gathered up her things and her daughter, and slipped away. It was like an episode of *Touched by an Angel.* I expected a dove to flutter through my kitchen and out the door.

I waited exactly the amount of time she told me, tested the loaves how she showed me, and set them to cool according to her careful instructions. The kids and I cut into one of them while it was still hot, slathered the slices with butter (because that's what we do in Texas ... we slather things), and ate. And ate. And ate.

Since that day I have been able to make pretty good bread on my own. I just needed a little help from someone who is gifted in that area. And interestingly, I got a teeny bit better at cooking other foods as well. Her tips didn't just help me with bread but gave me an understanding of how to mix ingredients and use some of my kitchen tools properly.

That day with my friend was almost twenty years ago, and my family is still reaping the benefits. She identified my problems and helped me learn how to overcome them. She kept saying to me while we mixed and kneaded, "It's nothing ... this is so easy!"

Uh-huh. Easy for YOU!

Your simple assignment:

1. Write down what you think are your three biggest problems.

2. Consider one way you are a cause of each of those problems, and take that up as a matter of prayer. (God wants to inspire you to change!)

3. Read James 1:2–8.

CHAPTER 4

Make the Connection

About ten years after we did that original kitchen remodel, the room started to look frayed around the edges. Plus, I love to change things up and paint the walls a new, updated color. So when our oldest daughter was about to graduate from high school with maybe a party and friends coming over, I knew it would be a good time to freshen the kitchen up once again. But in a much simpler way ... no new floors or cabinets. Just some touch-ups and maybe, just maybe, a new fridge. But how to break the idea to my husband?

Being homeschoolers, we had options for her graduation. We tossed several ideas around and finally settled on the idea of formally graduating her, so we planned a small ceremony with dinner and outdoor games afterward. We would have the event in our front yard and invite about seventy-five people.

About six weeks before the date, I said to James, "Honey, we really need to redo the kitchen before this party. It's so outdated, several things are broken, and it doesn't meet all of our needs. Let's talk about giving it a small makeover."

He was not thrilled with the idea. He brought up trivial facts like we had no time or money.

But I was a woman on a mission, and I was determined to find some way. As is often the case when I suggest a project, he explained to me that it was unlikely we could do it, but I should go ahead and put together a budget and we would talk about it (this man is *very* patient with me). I drew upon my strengths and sketched out my dreams for the kitchen, shopped for materials, and made calls to check prices. I assembled a detailed list (I know details make him happy) and invited him to dinner so we could discuss it.

Doesn't every man love to talk with his wife about spending money while dining at a nice restaurant?

He was happy to have dinner with me, but he wasn't going for my kitchen plans. He politely went through my proposal line by line, and the longer we talked the more reality sank in. We just couldn't swing it. Money was really tight, and the cost of the graduation party was already weighing on us.

But my dream of hosting and making people comfortable felt like it hinged on having crown molding and a fridge big enough to hold two cakes from Costco.

It wasn't all for the party, of course. Our kitchen had been needing an update for a long time. The party just gave me a deadline. Every day as the kids made their lunches, it was like a seven-car pileup since we had very little counter space, and the fridge really didn't hold everything we needed as our family grew. The cabinets were desperate for a coat of paint, and the list went on. And on.

He didn't disagree that we needed to do some work on the kitchen, but he stood his ground that we couldn't spend any money on it at the time. So I had a problem.

Not agreeing with your spouse is a big part of what makes marriage hard. You have your idea of what you want your life to look like, and he has his. When you were courting, it was more about feelings and passion and not much talk about who would empty the dishwasher or do middle-of-the-night diaper changes.

But once the honeymoon wore off, the reality of merging two lives together set in. After twenty-nine years together, James and I are just beginning to figure it out. Part of the solution to my problem is making what is important to him important to me.

If you're familiar with the Dave Ramsey teaching that there is a free spirit and a nerd in every relationship, then you won't have any trouble figuring out which is me and which is James. It could seem like an impasse, but thankfully I figured out somewhere along the way that his nerdiness is actually a gift to me. If left to myself I would fritter around doing fun projects and making the world beautiful while draining our bank account and burying us in debt. On the flip side, he needs this free-spirit wife to pull him out of his all-logic-and-no-play mentality. Man cannot live on logic alone!

God made us different so that we would be strong where the other is weak. And that, my beautiful friends, is a gift we all too often overlook.

OPERATING IN THE FLOW

We do the same with all our problems. We see them as something to get rid of instead of something that can grow us.

I once heard a story about a man who lived in a house on a hill. There was a huge rock right outside his front door, as tall as he was and twice as wide. One night God told the man, "Tomorrow, go out there and push the rock with all your might." The man protested because the rock was so huge, but he finally gave over to follow God's instruction.

Day after day the man pushed and pushed on that rock. He began to feel hopeless because the rock never moved, no matter how hard he pushed. Finally, after months of pushing on the rock, the man cried out to God, "It is impossible! *Why* do you have me doing this when I can never move the rock?"

God smiled down on the man and replied, "You have done well. You think you failed because the rock didn't move, but I told you only to push on the rock. I could have moved it myself, but that was not the goal. Now, look at your muscles. You are stronger than you ever were before. Stop pushing the rock and go lift your brother's burdens."

There are many versions of this story, but in this one we are reminded that our goal is not always God's goal. Even when we are following His direction we must not assume we understand His purpose.

Lysa TerKeurst calls it operating in the flow:

> Operating *in the flow* of God's power is so much better than working *against the flow* of God's power. Seeking to obey God in the midst of whatever cir-cumstance I'm facing is what positions me to work in the flow of God's power. I still have to navigate the realities of my situation, but I won't be doing it in my own strength. My job is to be obedient to

God, to apply His Word, and to walk according to His ways—not according to the world's suggestions. I want to participate in His divine nature rather than wallow in my own bad attitude and insecurities.[1]

We can look at all our personal challenges as opportunities to grow and fulfill God's purposes in a way we did not imagine! And we're ready to tap into what we have already learned about ourselves to build an arsenal of tools we can use to turn our struggles around.

Since we have already established the fact that we can find solutions to our problems by adjusting something about ourselves, how do we tap into that? Here's where our gifts and talents and dreams merge with our problems. Our problems are the struggle, and our talents and vision are the way through them. How about that?

PROJECT TIME!

Let's go back and look at your lists from the first three chapters. Get a piece of paper and draw three columns. Over the first column write "Gifts," over the next write "Dreams," and over the last write "Problems." Now write down the three to five things you had on each list. This is your jumping-off point to start finding joy and victory in the midst of what you are dealing with.

Once you have your three columns ready, draw a line—like a three-year-old with an activity book—to connect one of the items in your problem list with something in the other two lists.

DO-OVER LIST

GIFTS	DREAMS	PROBLEMS

GRATITUDE

If you need to, you can make longer lists. You have more than five gifts and dreams ... I know you do! Or write down the main problem you are dealing with and then everything you can think of that would apply in the first two lists. Then connect.

Let's try an example. One issue many women deal with is fatigue. It can range from postpartum tiredness to having been sick lately to serious health issues. But no matter what the cause, being fatigued can cause plenty of problems.

You can't get your work done; you can't help the kids when they need it; you have trouble keeping up with commitments—these are just some among many other issues. While you work on your health and look for ways to tackle the fatigue, you can look at your list and see what help God gave you to draw from until you can, hopefully, get rid of the problem altogether.

If nothing jumps out at you right away, take one of the things on your list and unpack it a little. If you love sports, what is it that you love? Being outside? Competition? Working with a team? Rules? Uniforms?

Now grab the detail that excites you and apply it to your problem. For example, in trying to overcome fatigue, infuse your love for working with a team in a creative way. You could make a game for the kids out of straightening their rooms, you could create a space to sit outside and watch the kids play, or you could build a competition with yourself to help you get things done. Make small goals and give yourself a point if you complete it before the time you allowed yourself.

If finances are your struggle, that is a great opportunity to tap into your gifts. Are you an artist? Use that to teach classes in your home, inviting the students to bring all of their own materials. If you adore reading, host an online book club using affiliate links for your members to buy the books. If you love healthy eating, make healthy menus every week and offer them to subscribers for one dollar. If you love to organize, offer to help friends organize their kitchens for a small fee or trade.

If you, like many of us, struggle in your marriage, use your talents and passions to turn that around. I love decorating. My husband isn't interested in that, so how could I use it to improve my marriage? By exploring what it is about decorating that would bless him. My husband, for instance, has some problems with his back and it hurts him to stand for long periods, so I make sure there's a comfortable chair in every room where he can sit, including the bathroom! Why not? He likes to hang out with me in the bathroom while I get ready in the morning, and I want him to be comfortable. His office is overflowing with tax books and law books and his clients' files. I am able to help him make the space work so everything fits and looks nice when clients come to meet with him. I can make sure he has room on his side of the bed and a place to charge his phone. All of that is meeting his needs by using my gifts.

Ask yourself, *What is it that I love most about _____ and how could that apply to _____?*

Most of all, pray over your lists. God gave you your amazing skills and passions. He knows everything you need to get through your struggles, and He will lead you to a place of hope. You are rich with inspiration and encouragement. You are amazing!

I'm inspired by this message from Jennie Allen in *Restless*:

> It's beautiful that your heart doesn't beat fast about the same things my heart beats over. It's beautiful that your gifts are not the same as your mom's, and your place is not the same as your best friend's. When we start to lay out our threads, it is unbelievable—breathtaking, really—to see how what felt average about ourselves weeks ago starts to take on intricate beauty. Our untangling threads reveal God's sovereignty and attention to detail. Beautiful is the body of Christ stretched and

poured out into every crevasse of this world, every
city, every neighborhood, every office, every home.
It's the unselfish passions of people displaying the
love of their God in a million unique ways.[2]

You are fearfully and wonderfully made!

Also, working within our talents gives us energy. You know how
you can be worn out from paying bills and think you are too tired to
add the numbers one more time, and then you get up and walk over
to something you enjoy doing, and suddenly you have the energy
to do it? That energy comes from your enthusiasm for the activity.
Knowing what you love helps you know how to bring joy back to
a difficult moment. Coffee lovers know what a simple, seemingly
insignificant cuppa joe can do for their day. They were dragging and
unfocused, and after half of their warm cup of goodness is consumed
they have a new energy. The Holy Spirit can do that same thing for
you. Drink Him in when you are emotionally dragging and can't
focus on the truth of the problem, and He will give you wisdom and
understanding that can fill you with an energy that is unexplainable.

What we have received is not the spirit of the world,
but the Spirit who is from God, so that we may understand what God has freely given us. (1 Cor. 2:12)

For those moments when joy seems far away, your premade list
of things you love can help. Before we spend too much time connecting columns, be sure you don't include sitting and mindlessly
entertaining yourself as a passion. There is a place for that, but it's not

a talent (although I do sometimes notice I am especially good at it). There is no real fulfillment in that. Rest and relax when you need to, but when the goal is to get past a problem, watching TV or pleasure reading won't help. You may have to force yourself to take some kind of action, even if it's simple. But you will feel so much better!

If you can't seem to find ways to link your talent list with your problem list, ask a friend for help. It's always so much easier to see through the muck of self-doubt on someone else's list. You could even do it as an exercise together or in a small group. Take turns reading one problem you have and giving a brief explanation. Then read your top three dreams or talents and let the others help you find ways to connect your columns.

And be open. Even if at first you disagree or are a little bit hurt by someone else's suggestion, just listen. Write down what she says and then take it home to pray about it. If it's useful, go with it. If not, just let it go. You are not obligated to follow through with anyone's suggestions, but by opening up to your friends, you are giving them a chance to use their skills and creativity to help someone else! And, as an added bonus, they have an extra layer of understanding about how to pray for you.

Your problems, your weaknesses, and your willingness to see that you are a part of your problems shows the world a great God who produces beautiful fruit through your trials.

MY DREAM KITCHEN

As our graduation party approached, James and I continued to talk about the kitchen makeover. I brought it up so often that he finally asked me one day, "Why is this so important to get done before the graduation?" The question stumped me. I thought about the best way to reply since he had never asked me this before. "Well," I said thoughtfully, "I want the party to flow smoothly, and frankly, since most of these guests may never come back to our house, I want to have it looking the best it can."

He mulled that over and then replied, "What about letting our friends see that we are the kind of people who don't remodel their kitchen if they can't afford it?"

Ouch!

That concept wouldn't get my kitchen remodeled! But it touched a spot in me. I did want to present myself as real and not something I wasn't. His question made me stop and evaluate what it was I was trying to do. I went back to the drawing board and decided to flip the question of budget back on him. "Okay, then let me ask you this: how much, if anything, do we have at our disposal to spend on fixing up the kitchen?"

He took a couple of days to crunch the numbers (that's what he does—he crunches numbers all day long and takes great care of our finances). He came back with a very small amount. But it surprised me because I expected him to say there was nothing.

I figured out a way, by cutting way back on the plans, to make that work. I could buy paint and some wood to build another cabinet, and if I sold a few things we had in storage, tightened up the grocery expenses, and shopped for a great deal, I could buy a fridge. It was actually fun. I got to tap into my gift for making junk look nice and organizing with scraps. I looked at the problems I had in my kitchen with fresh eyes and figured out ways to make it better within the boundaries.

I discovered new layers to my dream of having a beautiful home, which included honoring my husband and being creative. I asked a couple of friends who were good at design to come look at my kitchen, listen to my plans, and see if they had any suggestions. One of them offered some brilliant ideas I never would have thought of, because she could see the whole picture so much better than I could.

In the end, we had just what we needed for our party, and the freshly painted and reorganized kitchen was functioning much better for our daily lunch routine. I loved how it turned out and even figured out a way to replace my island countertop for less than forty dollars. The whole thing was a labor of love, and as an added bonus, none of it was so valuable that I ever need to worry that the kids will ruin it.

I would have never even thought of that little extra blessing.

Whatever your problem is, big or small, there is an answer. It will likely *not* be the answer you want. But that is when you get to try out those talents and dreams and become something bigger than your dreams. That is when you get to dig into a new and improved you that shines a light on how generous and merciful our God is.

Your simple assignment (since we did some work in the chapter!):

1. Follow instructions in this chapter for connecting the three columns.

2. Show the chart to your spouse or a close friend and ask for his or her insight.

3. Prayerfully decide which problem you want to tackle first.

4. Read Mark 11:20–25.

CHAPTER 5

The Plan

Suppose one of you wants to build a tower. Won't you first sit down and estimate the cost to see if you have enough money to complete it? For if you lay the foundation and are not able to finish it, everyone who sees it will ridicule you, saying, "This person began to build and wasn't able to finish." (Luke 14:28–30)

I am not naturally a plan maker. When I run with my natural instincts, I tend to dive right into projects without a hair of a plan, believing it will all turn out fine in the end. I have been in plenty of tight spots as a result of my tendency not to prepare. I am thinking specifically of the deck I built in my backyard one summer that swayed dramatically to the left if anyone actually tried to step on it.

When we were first married, I had no idea how to organize anything. One day James asked me to clean out the pantry because it was hard to find what we needed. He then happily left for work, thinking it was a simple request and I would be fine. I stood there staring at the mess, wishing I could just throw it all away and start over. All day long I tried to get it more organized, and by the time he got home from work that evening I was on the kitchen floor crying, surrounded by cans of green beans and baking supplies.

"What's wrong?" he asked. (Don't you feel sorry for those poor new husbands who have no idea what they are getting themselves into?) I tearfully explained that I couldn't figure out how to organize the pantry. He started to laugh. Big mistake.

Once he managed to get me to come out of the bathroom he showed me some simple tips. He had me make three piles: one for keeping, one for giving away (or putting somewhere else), and one for throwing away. Okay, I could do that. I made my piles. Then he showed me how to divide the keep pile into whatever categories I wanted (canned fruit, crackers, oils, baking supplies, and so on), which would help me see how much shelf space each category needed. Once I did that, I could see how to set it all up inside the tiny pantry, and the rest, as they say, is history.

IT'S EASIER THAN YOU THINK

We make plans for our goals in much the same way. First, decide what it is you want to accomplish. Next, figure out what is required to get that done, and then put those tasks in order.

Let's say you want to make a flower arrangement for the centerpiece at a dinner you are hosting. That's your goal. First you have to decide what you need in order to make that happen. You don't need to figure out the order yet—just make a list. You need to get some flowers, find something to put them in, decide what color you want and how much you can spend, locate a place to actually make the arrangement, and gather the tools you will need to make it.

Once you have your list, put it in order. I might first choose my container so I know what size the flowers should be. Then I will get out my tools in case there's anything I don't have. I'll make a list of what flowers to get and where/when to buy them, set aside a certain time and place to arrange them, and voilà! I'm done with my plan. The options might change as I begin the task, but the goal is to have the plan, and then you can adapt as necessary.

Of course, most of our goals and problems are much less defined. We want a healthier marriage or well-behaved kids or to be able to take a shower without interruption. Maybe you are feeling lonely or depressed, and it is hard to make a clear plan for that kind of issue. But it is possible!

I want you to go back to the chart you made and find the bottom section below the horizontal line. Underneath where you have connected your columns, start making a list of things you need in order to accomplish the goal of dealing with those problems. Be free with your thoughts. You don't need to actually have it all … just write freely. You can be as practical or as imaginative as you want. The one rule is that you can write only things that you have control over. No writing things like, "Make my husband more romantic." In that case you would write something like, "Find ways to be satisfied with the romance my husband offers."

If your problem is that little Johnny won't be still when you're putting him into his car seat, write things like, "Be confident in my mothering," and "Look for ways to teach Johnny to obey me when we are at home to support the message that he has to do what I tell him." Think of what you need to accomplish this task. Maybe you need to bring his car seat in the house and practice in a controlled environment when you aren't in a hurry. Think outside the box.

I encourage you to ask your husband for ideas. Men often have thoughts that are so opposite of how we think that at first they seem ridiculous to us. But go ahead and write them down anyway. God can use those ideas to spark something else in you and help you figure out what you need to move past your problems. The two of you were meant to work together.

Now that you have your ideas, just let them settle on you for a bit of time. If you're like me and like to get things done quickly, you may need only an hour or two. If you like to let things steep, give it a few days. Then go back and look at your list. Circle what you still think may work as a plan for overcoming your problem, and add anything else you have thought of.

Often once we start the wheels turning, they begin to roll, and we can't stop ourselves from seeing a new angle or opportunity in our situation. Sort out the useful ideas, and ask God to turn the crazier ones into something you can work with.

Let's review all we have done so far with a sample problem.

If I have a problem with getting my boys to clean their rooms each morning, here's what I would do. In my gifts column, I would write a few of my talents that might apply to the problem: photography, room arranging, and being slightly OCD (it's a gift, believe it or not). In my dream column, I would write what I would have in a perfect world: a neat home, children who do what they are asked, and the ability to get things done on time. Lastly, the problem: my boys don't clean their room as expected.

Below those columns I would write all the things that are needed to get past this problem: I should be better about checking it after they have cleaned it, making sure it is clean when they go to bed, making sure they understand what is expected of them, making it easier for them to do, finding ways to motivate them, and making sure they know I love them anyway.

Now I can sit down with my husband (and the boys too if I wanted) and make a solid plan.

1. Clean the room with the boys and help them see where everything goes (room arranging).

2. Get rid of things they don't need or use to make it less cluttered.

3. Label where things belong (OCD).

4. Take a picture of the clean room and hang it on the back of their door for them to reference (photography).

5. Check their room with them at night when putting them to bed so it's less of a job in the morning (OCD).

6. Have them ask me to check it before they can eat breakfast (showing them they are loved).

7. Give them praise for their efforts (more love).

Now I have a plan. Things will change, and it's likely I will have to come up with more ideas to motivate them as they get lazy or have their own struggles. But I am no longer going into every morning frustrated and hopeless and yelling at my kids because things aren't going my way.

I find that, through the act of making my plans, the clouds of confusion and doubt almost always start to disappear. I am able to see my situation with less emotion, and that clears my thoughts and gives me confidence.

You aren't always going to be able to make your problems go away, but you will have tools for how to better manage them. These tools will help you with all life's struggles, from messy rooms to depression to divorce. There is always something you can do to help you get through it and have joy!

And be sure to write your plan down. Don't worry; it's not going to be chiseled in stone. You will definitely need to alter things about it and reevaluate often. It takes time to get out of old habits and create new ones. It takes courage to keep trying.

RESHAPING

When I started my weight-loss journey, one book that helped me was *Reshaping It All* by Candace Cameron Bure. She has a great perspective on the verse in Luke that I quoted at the beginning of this chapter:

> In that passage Jesus was pointing out the cost of being a disciple. Life will offer us a thousand and one reasons we shouldn't follow Christ, but those who have built their faith on conviction won't give up because they have counted the cost beforehand

and their eyes are fixed on the goal ahead. The same principle should apply to the important life goals we set. We consider the pros and cons *before* we start; then we map out a reasonable plan and stick to it.[1]

When you want to solve a problem or make changes in your life, making a plan is vital. If what we have been talking about were a body, your dream is the heart and the problem is the disease. The plan, then, is the blood that carries the white blood cells (my apologies to any medical professionals reading this).

A plan carries your vision to overcome a problem into action.

If I just walked into my kitchen one day with a sledgehammer and knocked out a few walls without a plan, I would not know if the fridge I wanted would fit or if the counter would cover a much-needed outlet. I could destroy something that would later be necessary for preparing our family meals.

It sounds so easy, right? Make a plan. But how do we make a plan for getting past those really rough days of mothering, marriage, and household responsibilities that seem to pile up faster than we can keep up with?

It is easier than you think. Let's tackle it together!

Step One: Pray

> Commit to the LORD whatever you do, and he will establish your plans. (Prov. 16:3)

The first thing on every list you will ever see me make is prayer. Pray, pray, pray. Talk to God. Ask for His help and wisdom and insight. Ask Him to give you the creativity you lack. Ask Him to give you the control you need. Ask Him to light the path so you know exactly where to step next.

It can be hard, especially when the kids are little, to find enough time to have long talks with God. That's okay! He knows you have babies, and He wants you to focus on them. If all you have is five minutes in the bathroom to give your thoughts fully to God, take advantage of it. When you sit down to write out your plans, breathe a prayer dedicating your thoughts to God. When you're driving, instead of calling your friend, call upon Him.

Prayer is not only for the purpose of seeking help. It is also giving God glory, asking for His will to be done, and asking forgiveness. So many things are wrapped up in that time with Him. And it's amazing how much it changes us! I often find that just the *act* of prayer gets me past a problem before I ever have to make a list or do anything else. Shauna Niequist puts it like this:

> The act and posture of prayer connects me back to something I lose so often, something that gets snipped like a string. Prayer ties up the string one more time. Prayer says, I know you're up there. I believe you. I can make it. I know you are good. To pray is to say that there is more than I can see, and more than I can do. There is more going on than meets the eye.[2]

Step Two: Become Saturated in Scripture

Before we can really know God's will for us (or anyone else), we must know what He has to say. Sure, we can hear from the Holy Spirit, but no internal word from God can ever go against what He has shown us already in His revealed Word. We must intentionally fill our minds and hearts with Scripture.

As I mentioned before, I am inspired by Elisabeth Elliot, and I have read her book *Keep a Quiet Heart* several times. In it she says this about God's Word:

> Mercifully, God does not leave us to choose our own curriculum. His wisdom is perfect, His knowledge embraces not only all worlds but the individual hearts and minds of each of His loved children. With intimate understanding of our deepest needs and individual capacities, He chooses our curriculum. We need only ask, "Give us this day our daily bread, our daily lessons, our homework."[3]

Read it daily, listen to it, put it to music, let the kids read it aloud, write it on your mirrors, post it on your fridge, and hang it over the mantle. Surround yourself with the wisdom that comes only from God!

Step Three: Prepare

If we are going on vacation, it's obvious that we have to plan. We have to prepare to take time off from work, make sure we have transportation, make arrangements for places to stay, pack our clothes, check our bank account—there are so many areas in which we must prepare. Even if we want to drive off carefree without a destination, we need gas, money, food, clothes, and so on.

But most of the time in our daily lives we don't think about making a plan. Our lives roll in and out of the same old thing day after day. Why do we need a plan for that? Because without an idea of how we are going to accomplish our goals, we will never get there.

It's like the book *If You Give a Mouse a Cookie*. In that book each thing you give the mouse makes him want something else. Give him a cookie, and "He's going to ask for a glass of milk. When you give him the milk, he'll probably ask you for a straw," and so on.[4] This is what it looks like to have no plans! You go in a circle until, at the end of the day, you are right where you started (or worse) … In the end, the little mouse asks for another cookie.

You already have a plan, even if you didn't make it purposely. What time you need to be at your meeting, how you'll get there, and what to feed the kids for breakfast are all part of how you prepare. With just a little bit of forethought, you would be a lot more likely to reach the goals you've set for the day.

As a free spirit, I love to go through my day being spontaneous and carefree. That's fine! I love that about myself. But it doesn't mean I should have no plans at all. You're not chiseling them in stone; you're simply creating a guide.

Step Four: Be Willing to Change

This is a weak area for me. Once I make a plan, I tend to get completely attached to it—so much that I am unwilling to change. I have been known to hold on to an idea so fiercely that if someone tries to alter it in any way, I practically turn it into World War III. Oh sure, I am spontaneous when it comes to a friend inviting me to lunch at the last minute. But if you try to get me to change the route I drive to church, you will have a fight on your hands.

But here's the amazing thing: when you make your plans and then let them go, that's where God takes over. Of course you need to know what steps to take to accomplish a goal. Of course you make that plan with study and experience and work. You pray, you make sure you're in line with the Bible, and you run it past your husband and good friends. Then you give it second place in your heart. You do your best and let God make the changes necessary to send you where you need to be. It must ultimately be His will that we seek.

C. S. Lewis (one of my all-time favorite authors) says in his book *Mere Christianity*:

> Imagine yourself as a living house. God comes in to rebuild that house. At first, perhaps, you can understand what He is doing. He is getting the drains right and stopping the leaks in the roof and so on; you knew that those jobs needed doing and so you are not surprised. But presently He starts knocking the house about in a way that hurts abominably and does not seem to make sense. What on earth is He up to? The explanation is that He is building quite a different house from the one you thought of—throwing out a new wing here, putting on an extra floor there, running up towers, making courtyards. You thought you were going to be made into a decent little cottage: but He is building a palace. He intends to come and live in it Himself.[5]

LEMME 'SPLAIN. NO, LEMME SUM UP

Making plans to accomplish a goal is not always a simple task. Some are easy … you want to make cookies, you find the recipe. Just go down the list of ingredients that someone else has put together, and follow the instructions. But when it is a more personal goal, like overcoming a trial, we have to figure it out ourselves.

I have given you much to work on in this chapter. You may be shooting for a huge change, like moving to a new house or altering your whole diet. (*Diet* is such a small word for such a huge impact—when I stopped eating sugar, I thought I wouldn't make it through the day. #addictionisbad) Or you may be trying to make small adjustments, like doing a better job of keeping the kitchen clean or getting through emails without it taking your entire day.

The process of making any kind of change is the same. Write it down, then pray, lean on Scripture, and prepare. And yes, be willing to change yourself, always. I don't want you to be over-whelmed by this! Don't try to become a completely different person. It will burn you out and you won't make it. Why not tackle one thing at a time? Do something small to start with, like keeping the kitchen counter free of clutter for two weeks (did I just hear a gasp?). That's not easy, but it is a small change. It might take all your energy to retrain your family not to drop everything there and leave it. Old habits die hard. Make your plan and share it with your family. Then stay on it. I promise it is possible, and you may discover that *you* are the toughest nut to crack when you find yourself continuing to set things down instead of putting them away like you envisioned. That's when you ask God for help. He cares about those little things because they make room for the good He wants to pour into your life!

Once you have created a new habit, move on to something else. You will be surprised at how much those little changes affect the bigger problems. Once your kids get the consistent message that nothing lands on the counter that doesn't belong there, they may just start doing that organically in other areas of the house. And even if that doesn't happen, you will be more peaceful just having that one victory, and you'll have more confidence for the next change you want to make.

You're not alone. God has perfect ideas. He is the author of all order and organization, and He will help you.

THE BRIGHT SIDE

As I forged ahead with my kitchen remodel, I continually altered the plans. No matter how hard I tried, there was always an unexpected obstacle that threw a wrench in the goal.

I had planned to rip out a built-in cabinet and add a small set of drawers with a cutting-board countertop. I needed a place for the kids to cut and more drawer space for their snacks. I was going to call it the lunch counter, and it was going to be perfect. Until I tore out the built-in only to find a ninety-year-old stone chimney that the cabinet had been built around. Right in the middle of my kitchen.

I was telling my husband that I wanted to take my favorite sledgehammer to the chimney and keep going with my plans.

He would not hear of it! He had fallen in love at first sight with the stone pillar and insisted we keep it. Rock, meet hard place. Hello.

After debating it for hours and hearing him talk about his grandmother's house and the chimney she had, combined with the look of fondness on his face when he talked about it, I knew there was no hope of me getting rid of that thing. I was stuck with the chimney and said a sad farewell to my lunch counter.

I altered my plans and built around the chimney (more foam core). Eventually it became the centerpiece of the kitchen and is still there today. Even though I don't love it as much as my husband does, I do love the character it gives the kitchen.

I also found a way to use a corner of the kitchen that I had set aside for a sitting area to make a smaller lunch counter. It turned out to be nice because it's on the opposite side of the room from where I had first planned, which means the kids are more spread out than they would have been with my original idea. Now that they're older and have adult-sized bodies, the space at lunch-prep time is a gift.

There's always, always, always a bright side.

Your simple assignment:

1. Commit to pray over your chart each morning for the next week.

2. Write down a first draft of a real plan for how to change one problem. (Hopefully you have some

inspiration by now, but if not, just forge ahead and it will work out fine.)

3. Read James 4:13–17.

CHAPTER 6

Making Changes

At some point in each of the kids' lives, I decide it's time to officially teach them how to cook. I don't mean just nachos and grilled cheese sandwiches but a genuine whole meal for the family. My first lesson is always on how to make soup. Soup is easy and more forgiving than other kinds of recipes (except casseroles, but we're not big fans of casseroles at our house).

I have a favorite recipe for black bean soup that I adapted from a cookbook back in the nineties. I serve it anytime we are having guests (if it's fall or winter) because it's almost foolproof. Or, as we like to call it, Lisa-proof. (If you want to make it, I've included the recipe at the end of the book!)

When one of my girls was thirteen, I realized we had not gotten around to her first real mother-daughter cooking class. So I told her to be ready to make dinner on Thursday. She looked a little bit panicked, but I assured her it would be fine. I would be helping her. That wasn't as reassuring as I had hoped.

On Thursday afternoon we stood side by side at the kitchen island, and I read the recipe to her. I called out each ingredient, and she gathered them from their places. My plan was to start by showing her how to chop each vegetable to the appropriate size for the soup.

She got flustered by the carrots, and no matter how many times I showed her how to keep them from rolling out from under her, they kept slipping and she eventually sliced her finger. It was a rough start, but we kept going.

Next we needed to heat the oil and sauté the chopped veggies. But as we stirred the sizzling veggies I heard a cry from the other room. I told her, "Just keep stirring, and I will be right back." It seemed like I was gone for only a minute, but by the time I returned, the kitchen was filled with smoke and the vegetables were black in the bottom of the pot. And she was crying.

It felt, to her, like her cooking career had ended before it began.

The rest of the lesson went on like that. Me teaching, her crying; me trying to help, her burning something. By the time the soup was simmering on the stove and we were cleaning up, I was wondering if there was a cooking school in the area I could send her to for the rest of her high school years.

FINDING YOUR FLEXIBILITY

Plans never go the way you think they will. Even if it's only slightly off course, there will be something you have to adapt to. The stove won't heat right, or you can't find the can opener. Sometimes it's as simple as desperately needing to go to the bathroom right when the recipe says to "stir constantly."

Once you make a plan to overcome a problem, you have to be flexible in carrying it out.

Part of making a plan is being ready with alternate ideas. It's like my GPS when I go off the route it has for me … recalculating. It's not a bad thing. The destination is the same, and though it may take a little longer, I will see new things along the way and maybe even find a blessing I didn't expect.

We can't always know when a problem is going to arise, and there is inevitably something unexpected about the way it hits. So we have to be ready to adjust. And when we are working with other people, as either part of the problem or part of the solution, flexibility can be a challenge in itself.

My husband is the least flexible person I have ever met. He can't touch his toes or twist around to reach anything behind him. He can't even bend at the waist enough to sit upright when his legs are straight. Really, sometimes I ask him to try touching his toes just for my own entertainment. I, while no Olympic gymnast, am able to place my palms on the floor without bending my knees. I do notice that the older I get the harder it is to do. So I got myself a stretch machine.

I discovered this machine in hotel fitness centers when I would travel. It uses the weight of your body to simply stretch your back, legs, shoulders, and so on. I love the feel of stretching and pulling the kinks out of my muscles. So I got one for my house, and I stretch on it every morning. James, however, hates using it. He can't bend enough to use it without hurting himself.

There is nothing wrong with either of us; we are just different. And our levels of flexibility are different. I try to understand (while giggling a little) that he bends in ways I don't. And I appreciate him for not thinking I am freakish as I enjoy the hard stretch of the machine every morning.

In a similar way, we approach problems and solutions individually, and when things go off course we each bend differently. When the original solution we came up with isn't as effective as we hoped, I may go all out with a whole new plan, and he may just reach a little beyond what we had originally decided to try. Neither is wrong; it's just different.

We have to work together and accept each other's opinions and ideas. Flexibility within flexibility. Now *that* is a stretch!

This is especially true when managing problems with kids. You know how it starts. Your little princess won't stay in her bed at night. You know it's going to happen. You have made your list of things you're good at and figured out ways to use those talents to your advantage in the situation. You have talked it over with your husband, and you have a solid plan.

But ... you have never tried this plan before, and you don't know for sure how she will respond. You must be ready to switch it up if need be.

You put her to bed and she gets up. Here you go ... into the deep waters of parenting. You put her back into bed without the drink of water she is begging for. The first part of your plan complete. Check. Then she gets up again. Repeat. Soon she figures out this isn't going to work, and she starts screaming. Um, wow. You've never heard her scream like that. It wasn't part of the plan.

You want to keep going and let her scream until she falls asleep. Your husband wants to go into her room and read to her until she falls asleep. Neither of these ideas was part of your original plan. Maybe he just doesn't stretch the same way you do. Work together to compromise, and then rework the plan for tomorrow. Maybe he can go read one story, and then you will release him to go to bed while you sit at her door.

Alter and adapt is the name of the game. You decided together to work on this tonight, and you are dedicated to it. Look over your plan of action, and stick to it the best you can. Get through the night and reevaluate tomorrow. Make a freshly inspired plan and try again. I promise, you *are* making an impact on the problem. And remember, there are no hard-and-fast rules to this parenting gig. It's a constant stream of do-the-best-you-can.

In their book *Simple Life*, Thom S. Rainer and Art Rainer talk about being flexible:

> The simple life requires flexibility. Life is not static. Therefore, your day will demand that changes are made to continue this pursuit of yours. The activities or nonactivities will need adjustments as you continue to experience this journey of life. This may happen tomorrow; it may happen next year. Who knows where or what God may do with you? Do not limit yourself. Adopt an attitude of flexibility.[1]

SUCCESS SUITCASE

Wouldn't it be lovely to be in control of our emotions all the time? If I could figure out how to do that and bottle it, I would be a bajillionaire. Or I would be a Vulcan (any other sci-fi fans out there?). Either way, it's not possible for us humans. Emotions are raw and unfiltered and often unmanageable. They can be high and they can be low, and we don't want to shoot for controlling them. Instead, let's aim to control the way we respond when they pop up. It is when emotions are running strong that we turn to the beautiful fruits that the Spirit gives us and we cling to those qualities.

Lysa TerKeurst explores raw emotions and offers this thought:

> We must bring all of our raw reactions under the authority and truth of Jesus Christ. Our best efforts at human reasoning and willpower can't tame what we say externally (exploding) or experience internally (stuffing). Self-effort alone can't tame the tongue and our raw emotions that run wild.[2]

Emotions are the center of what gets in our way when we are trying to fix a problem we are having. If I decide to improve my marriage by being content with my husband's flaws, that seems like a good idea. I'll be doing okay until he does something that really hurts my feelings, and then I plummet. All those nasty emotions, like being angry and bitter, rise straight to the surface, and my plan for contentment goes out the window.

That's why we have to decide beforehand how we will behave. I will decide to smile and show love for him even when I am hurt. I won't lash out but, instead, will ask God for peace and kindness that can come only from Him. I may later share with my husband what hurt my feelings, but if my goal is to find joy, then I can't let what I am feeling in the moment stop that.

When dealing with your emotions, keep in mind that tomorrow you will probably feel differently. Prayer, sleep, time, exercise, or a good meal all can help. You don't want to be acting on your emotions.

because they are not trustworthy and will set you back in accomplishing your goals.

The entertainment industry feeds the idea that we should live by our emotions. A woman with a loveless marriage meets a guy who is sweet to her, and we are encouraged by the filmmaker to cheer that relationship on. Movies can make us sympathize with a murderer or root for a liar through editing and great storytelling. Then we carry that over into our own lives and become discontent with what we have. I encourage you to be careful with what you allow yourself to watch and read. And when you do see something that tells a story of following your heart, go home and examine it under the microscope of Scripture and truth so that you don't get lost in the sea of believing we should do what our heart tells us.

In *Reshaping It All*, Candace Cameron Bure (who has spent most of her life in Hollywood) has this to say:

> Pop culture would have us believe that by "following our heart" we can never go wrong. This is why it's so important that we dig into Scripture and keep digging. Because when we do, we discover that it is our job as stewards of this human vessel to guide ourselves with wisdom according to truth.[3]

She backs up her point by referring to Jeremiah 17:9, which says, "The heart is deceitful above all things and beyond cure. Who can understand it?"

As you begin to put your plans for getting through your struggles into action, think of it as packing a suitcase. What do you need for this journey of success? Start with your list, and then add the fruits of the Spirit: love, joy, peace, patience, kindness, goodness, faithfulness, gentleness, and self-control (Gal. 5:22–23). Wow! That's quite a task and one you cannot do on your own.

As you pack joy into your suitcase, ask God to help you use that when you need it. As you fold kindness into your plans, pray for ways to turn your heart in that direction exactly at the perfect time. Putting those fruits into your strategy will not only help guide you but will also redirect your responses.

The fruit of the Spirit of patience often doesn't make sense if we are following our hearts. But it is a gift to yourself that is more valuable than a cute pair of comfortable shoes. We get these terrible ideas in our heads that we should be able to conquer issues in one or two sessions. We think something isn't working because the next day we have the problem again.

Look back at your efforts and see what you learned. Recognize where you had success and where you need to mix it up. Just because you don't get instant results doesn't mean you're not succeeding. Sometimes making changes requires patience.

Maybe your idea needs tweaking. Maybe it needs a total over-haul. Or maybe you just need to give it a little time. If you see any changes in your situation, wait. Give it a few days (or more). It could be that you just need to show consistency.

Keep in mind that when dealing with an issue with your kids, they have a plan too, and it usually is the opposite of yours. You want her to stay in bed, and she wants to *not* stay in bed. But you have the advantage of being organized and prayerful, and you have wisdom and maturity that your child lacks. In fact, it is through seeing and experiencing your wisdom that she will learn what it looks like and begin to have it for herself. She may have been born smart, but she wasn't born wise. That comes from God, and He gives it to us through His Word and experience.

Just because it takes her some time to become convinced that her plan is not going to work doesn't mean you are failing. Hang in there, and decide to be patient and content.

The fruit of gentleness is a beautiful one! I could really use this most of the time. I can forge full steam ahead into a situation that calls for a more gentle approach. Then I end up hurting someone's feelings or being insensitive and making my problem (and hers) much worse. Being gentle toward others is a great thing to add to any list you are making when deciding how to handle a rough situation.

EXPECTING THE UNEXPECTED

Managing your expectations is another important part of the process. You certainly should expect to see results, but they won't usually look the way you imagined.

C. S. Lewis, in his book *Letters to Malcolm*, shares these thoughts about our expectations:

> It seems to me that we often, almost sulkily, reject the good that God offers us because, at that moment, we expected some other good. Do you know what I mean? On every level of our life—in our religious experience, in our gastronomic, erotic,

aesthetic, and social experience—we are always harking back to some occasion which seemed to us to reach perfection, setting that up as a norm, and depreciating all other occasions by comparison. But these other occasions, I now suspect, are often full of their own new blessing, if only we would lay ourselves open to it. God shows us a new facet of the glory, and we refuse to look at it because we're still looking for the old one.[4]

Be careful how you measure success. You can't measure your success by someone else's reaction. If making someone happy is your idea of a goal, you need to change that. If wanting your daughter to be *glad* to stay in bed is your mission, that will be difficult. You can't control other people's feelings or dreams. You can, however, have your own joy about the situation and not let yourself get discouraged. Others will see that, and even if they don't show it, they will want that same joy. They may think they can have joy only if they get what they want, but you know that's not true for them any more than it's true for you. Joy is not a result of circumstances; it is a result of having a relationship with the Holy Spirit and living a life of sacrifice and glory.

So don't make it your goal to have a happy child or happy husband. In the case of your husband, make it your goal to bless him and honor him. Show him the joy you have because you are married to him, and let that minister to him. How he responds is up to him, and you can't control that. (I know I wouldn't want someone else to try to control *me* like that!)

One book I LOVE is called *Boundaries*. In it, Dr. Henry Cloud and Dr. John Townsend explain how to know what you can really change:

> You can work on submitting yourself to the process and working with God to change you. You cannot change anything else: not the weather, the past, the economy—and especially not other people. *You cannot change others.* More people suffer from trying to change others than from any other sickness. And it is impossible.[5]

Putting your careful plan into action is risky because you are daring to try something different. You reached beyond what felt normal and comfortable for yourself and are willing to stretch. I am so proud of you for that. You will be shocked and surprised at what comes out of your efforts. It may well not be what you expected, but if you are ready for God to intercede, He will fulfill your dreams more than you could have imagined for yourself.

Can you be flexible? Can you accept the obstacles and react with kindness?

I want to stress here that you won't always change your surroundings. Sometimes they just are what they are. Sure, you can probably change your child's bedtime habits, but you are unlikely to be able to change the way your mother-in-law treats you or how hard it is to pay the bills at the end of the month.

It's so important to know that you aren't always trying to change the circumstances. Sometimes you are just working on yourself and altering your response to the difficulties.

BEAUTY FROM ASHES

The Thursday night after my daughter's first cooking lesson could have been dreadful. It certainly had all the signs of a doomed meal. But it was actually one of the sweetest memories I have.

She and I knew that the soup was not going to taste as good as it usually did. We had eaten this soup many times before, so the family was going to expect its usual goodness and be disappointed. My daughter didn't want to come to the table. She wanted to stay in her room without dinner. But I insisted that she come join us.

I told her that even though it got all messed up, her effort and work were the same as if it had turned out perfectly. The family was going to be thankful for how hard she worked, and they would want to share it with her and show their appreciation. As I told her this I prayed in my head, *Lord, please help them not say too much about how bad it is.*

We all sat down and everyone knew she had made the soup, but I announced it anyway. She sat in her place and was hanging her head low, not saying much. I set a steaming bowl of soup at each person's place, and after we prayed they began to eat. They all said, "Mmmmm ... I love this soup," as they spooned it into their mouths. My husband bragged at how hard it must be to make soup, and one of the other girls told how she had never been able to make this soup as well as this. As everyone ate, my daughter started to sit up straighter and tell the stories of how she cut her hand and burned the veggies and all of the other catastrophes that went with the meal preparations that day. She told them as if they were funny and smiled at me secretly as she left out the parts about crying and not wanting to sit at the table while the others tasted it.

I was so proud of my family that day. That pot of soup was the worst thing I have ever tasted. It was borderline inedible, yet everyone ate down to the bottom of their bowls, and some of the boys asked for more (probably to keep it from becoming leftovers).

My daughter knew it was awful too; there was no doubt about it. But she ate it and smiled, and no one ever said a word about it tasting perfectly horrid.

I had a plan to teach my daughter how to make soup, but God had a completely different plan. He wanted to show her that no matter how much she messes up, her family loves her and will do anything for her. That has been a gift to her as she has walked the tough road of the teen years—one I could never have taught her on my own.

Your simple assignment:

1. Which fruit of the Spirit is the hardest for you? Ask God each morning to help you clearly see opportunities throughout the day to work on that attribute.

2. Think of one way you are being stubborn in your plan. Ask God to help you be more flexible.

3. Read Romans 12:1–2.

CHAPTER 7

Joy

When I was almost nine months pregnant with baby number eight, I got a nesting bug that wouldn't quit. I was unstoppable with the organizing and cleaning and vacuuming weird places like the ceilings and outside walkway. There was one place I could not, no matter how much I tried, get clean. The kitchen floor.

I had a deep urge to scrub every inch of that floor, including under the fridge and behind the stove. But every time I tried to get it done, something would happen with the kids and I would get distracted.

I mentioned to James that I really, really needed to get that (and a few other things) done before I had the baby or I couldn't feel settled. This wasn't his first rodeo. He has experienced the wrath that is pregnant Lisa with dirty floors. So he offered, "The kids and I will get out of the house all day on Saturday, and you can have the whole place to yourself. You can clean all you want and even take a nap. And you know what? I will even take care of dinner so you can relax all evening."

Now, before you start offering him husband-of-the-year awards, read on …

Saturday morning came, and he and the kids found their shoes and headed out the door with a picnic lunch and giggles of excitement. I had no idea what they had planned, and I didn't ask. I knew better than that. It would only make me start trying to control their time together and worry about them, so I just smiled and waved as they marched out of the house.

I went immediately to my bathroom and took a long shower. I washed my face, clipped my nails, and got all ready for the part I had been looking forward to all week … the kitchen-floor scrubbing.

I waddled into the kitchen and set out all of my cleaning supplies. I rolled the fridge and oven away from the wall and started sweeping. Once it was sufficiently ready, I got on my hands and knees, wedged myself behind the fridge, and with my bucket of soapy water began to scrub. I had praise music playing through the house, and just about the time I was moving on to the stove, I heard a knock at the kitchen door. My music was really loud, so at first I wasn't sure what it was. Then I heard the telltale sound: "MOMMY! WHERE ARE YOU?"

What? No! It had been only an hour … were they back already? Panic. Freeze. Thoughts of staying behind the stove and hiding crossed my mind. I had just begun my plans for the day. I still wanted a NAP!

I heaved my enormously pregnant body out from behind the range just in time to see my older daughter lead my two-year-old away from the kitchen's french door. But the baby had spotted me already. And he was crying.

I opened the door and went out to see what was going on. At that same moment my husband was stepping out of his office (he works in a separate building behind our house). "Go back inside!"

he yelled to me. "It's your day off. The kids are fine. I told them not to bother you!"

Told them not to bother me? Say whuh? I stood there, looking around and taking in the situation. Ever so slowly I realized what was happening. He never planned to take them anywhere. He had actually locked the children *out* of the house and told them to play in the backyard all day while he worked and watched them from his office.

Oh my stinkin' goodness. I was positively dumbfounded.

How could I possibly relax now? Now that I knew my babies were actually mostly unattended and locked out of the house all day long, I would never be able to go forward with my plans. Why do men not understand this concept?

CHOOSING JOY

Every time our expectations get derailed, we have a choice. To move forward with joy or to go into a fuss and get mad. We can fight what God wants us to learn from the changes, or we can give over to a peace that, not to be cliché, passes understanding. We can be controlled by our immediate reaction, or we can stop and give it thought and purpose.

When you are trying so hard to stop yourself from lashing out in anger toward your child, where does your strength come from? That boiling, steaming, seemingly irresistible rage that explodes and then makes us blame our child … it is the opposite of joy!

We can get set off by the smallest of happenings. A child who won't cooperate or a slow line at the bank can turn us into a bad example of how to handle it when we don't get our way. I've seen people cursing the driver in front of them, and I wonder, is wherever they are going important enough to be cursing another person, even if that person is being careless? I know that when I act badly to other drivers I am contributing to the general notion that the world revolves around me and anyone who gets in my way be damned.

If I stop to give it any thought, I know that I have been the one who drives carelessly sometimes. I accidentally cut in front of someone or forget to signal a turn. I inconvenience other drivers and do things that could make them angry. I deserve no better treatment than I dish out when I am on the other side of that problem. So what if I decide to treat everyone I meet in traffic with kindness? Would that make a difference in the world? I think it would.

Every reaction is a choice. Even when we feel like we don't have a choice in how we behave, we do. To put it plainly, if we don't make purposeful decisions, we are left to our sin. Galatians 5:19–21 says, "The acts of the flesh are obvious: sexual immorality, impurity and debauchery; idolatry and witchcraft; hatred, discord, jealousy, fits of rage, selfish ambition, dissensions, factions and envy; drunkenness, orgies, and the like. I warn you, as I did before, that those who live like this will not inherit the kingdom of God."

When I am really willing to step out of my comfort zone and see myself, it is as plain as the nose on my face: I must not live simply by my sinful (natural) desires.

Making your list and checking it twice are the beginning to becoming dedicated to turning your struggles around. But at some point you will have to accept that you are choosing how you respond in the struggle. We have talked about our attitude and how we need to work on recognizing that we can make a difference by taking our part of the responsibility for the problem. But this choice goes much deeper.

This is about choosing joy when things get hard—when your child gets bullied or your bank account is empty or your husband locks your children out of the house. It is not an easy prospect. But God promises it is possible: "Consider it pure joy, my brothers and sisters, whenever you face trials of many kinds, because you know that the testing of your faith produces perseverance. Let perseverance finish its work so that you may be mature and complete, not lacking anything" (James 1:2–4).

In *Keep a Quiet Heart*, Elisabeth Elliot has this to say about trials:

> Everything about which we are tempted to complain may be the very instrument whereby the Potter intends to shape His clay into the image of His Son—a headache, an insult, a long line at the check-out, someone's rudeness or failure to say thank you, misunderstanding, disappointment, interruption.[1]

I don't want us to *pretend* we are joyful and bury our anger. Let's find the true joy that comes from the Holy Spirit so that it can make a permanent change in us, our families, and the people God places in our paths. This kind of joy cannot be an emotion, because emotions are uncontrollable and temporary. They are extensions of circumstances, good or bad, and they are gone tomorrow or the next time circumstances change.

Elliot goes on to add, "Wouldn't our children learn godliness if they saw the example of contentment instead of complaint? acceptance instead of rebellion? peace instead of frustration?"[2]

Depending on your personality and temperament, you may be more naturally joyful than I am. I'm more of a glass-half-empty kind of girl. But God has shown me in my weakness that He fills that glass to overflowing with an endless supply of what I need to trust in Him, regardless of what I see in front of me.

There are many times in every day that we face the choice: to be joyful despite the situation we are in, or to be defeated. Defeat leads to laziness, yelling, anger, hostility, [insert your tendency here]. But there is a way, through Christ, to overcome those inner battles and move forward through our troubles with continued joy.

Even one person with a joyful spirit can change the world. Wishing people well, showing concern for their troubles, letting them ahead of you in line … there are so many ways to spread love and gentleness instead of grumpiness and disrespect.

Personally, I want to be someone who spreads joy wherever I go. I know I fail miserably at this many times, but it is still my goal. Every time I mess up I learn. And I am forgiven. I develop a deeper love for others and an ability to communicate joy to them and inspire joy in them.

If you have been praying like we have talked about so much in previous chapters, then you will feel conviction when you treat others badly. If you don't, get back on your knees and ask God to show you where you need to change in order to become someone who lights up a room with joy. It all starts inside you. And you won't believe the delight you will experience from setting aside your mission and your "rights" involving the people around you. I know you may think you do that every day, but if you are fussing inside about the things that are making your life difficult, then you are really just hiding the truth of your own selfishness.

If you're looking for a place to begin making the change toward having a life filled with joy, start with gratitude. Take a look around you and find three things you are grateful for. There are plenty of books with great inspiration about being grateful. One of them, Ann Voskamp's *One Thousand Gifts: A Dare to Live Fully Right Where You Are* is filled with ways to show gratitude. I am inspired by her attitude: "Joy is the realest reality, the fullest life, and joy is always *given*, never grasped. God *gives* gifts and I *give* thanks and I unwrap the gift given: *joy*."[3]

FINDING JOY

At the end of the chapter, I am going to have you get that list back out again.

You have written down your problems, your gifts, your plan. Now draw another horizontal line below your plan notes, and write three things you are grateful for in the situation. Say anything ... list more than three if you want. God is working out something good for you in every problem. Being grateful for that is a place to start if you can't think of anything else.

After you make your list and you have prayed, go a little further and do some praising. Real, I-love-you-Lord kind of stuff. Find music that takes you to the mountaintop and crank it up. Raise your hands (be alone if you have to) and lift your chin. Give it your all. Sing. Hold your arms out to your side so your whole body is opened up. Thank Him for everything He has done for you and is doing for you and will do for you. For some of you this will feel awkward. That's okay. He meets you wherever you are. Your praise doesn't have to look like anything but you.

We always remember to praise Him in the good times, but doing it in the struggles is when it really makes a difference. You need to show yourself and the people around you that you trust Him no matter what is happening. Believe that your problems have a solution, and step out in faith that you will be better off because of them.

Joy doesn't always look like peppy, giddy happiness. It can be quiet and still.

When our youngest son was two years old, we had a very difficult situation come up. I wrote a post on my blog with some ideas we were using for training him, and some very hateful women found it and decided that my parenting choices were abusive. They got a group together and actually called the police. (I had never met any of these women, and as far as I know they didn't even live in my state!) In fact, a bunch of them called within a few hours and that raised a red flag, I am sure, at the police station. Thankfully we were alerted that it was happening and were prepared when the police arrived at our door early the next morning.

What transpired after that was an eight-month-long nightmare of being investigated and harassed. Not only was there the possibility of losing our son, but I received several death threats. We immediately had to alter our lifestyle to protect our family.

But even then there were things every day that I found joy in. That first day when we faced a very hostile policeman at the front door, I felt a strong sense of peace. We had been up praying all night, and God not only prepared us with an understanding of our legal rights but also led me into a place of comfort that I had never felt before. I was so filled with joy that I never lost trust that He would take loving care of us. I had no promise of victory or the kind of success I hoped for, but I had an assurance that He would hold us all in His loving arms no matter what happened. (We were completely vindicated in this situation, and all charges were erased.)

I woke up every day and chose to find joy. The kind of joy you experience when you are in the middle of something very difficult is different from what you feel when life is smooth. It is earned. It is a medal of honor pinned to your heart by a King who adores you. It is quiet and still and everything magnificent.

A TINY PEACE

The funny thing is that sometimes it is actually harder to find joy and peace in the small things. When you're in a really hard battle, people are praying for you, and you are remembering to equip yourself each day for the rough road ahead. But during everyday, ordinary situations, you forget. You wake up to the baby crying and don't get back into your room to get dressed for the next four hours because you are constantly putting out little fires. Something spills, someone bumps his head, one of the kids sneaks outside, and a friend calls to see if she can stop by to pick up the book you borrowed from her a year ago—and you have no idea where it is.

You just can't get a handle on the day. It gets away from you, and joy is the last thing on your mind. You're mostly thinking about coffee. And putting the kids in front of the TV.

And those kinds of days, the plain, painful, lost ones when you feel like your life is being wasted and no one thinks about you, is what this book is really about. I want to minister a kind of joy to you, moms in the trenches, that you can have right there. Right now. Simple, pure, everyday joy.

You will have to be determined. But you are so strong. I know you don't feel like it most of the time. I have been there! But that girl who had dreams and plans for her life and passions for her future is not lost.

Take a look back at your lists from the first two chapters. See her? The girl who loved life? Who wanted to be a ballerina? An artist? A writer? Let her out!

In *Restless,* Jennie Allen embraces the knowledge that God is leading us even through the simplest of moments:

> God is accomplishing a thousand tiny purposes at any given moment around us. There is only so much we can know, but we can leave stuff we can't know to God, and believe He has it all worked out. It may feel quiet, and we possibly even feel forgotten, but God is moving to work out His plans all around us. What is our part? Trust.[4]

Do you trust Him? Do you have confidence that He will fill your stressful days with joy even if nothing else changes?

It starts at the beginning of the day. Wake up, and before you do anything else, give thanks. You have time for that. Even if a baby is lying next to you crying, you can take ten seconds to say, "Thank You,

God, for this beautiful day!" With each step you take, look for things to be grateful for. Thank Him for a flushing toilet, a husband who works hard for your family, the children He gave you, your house, food on your table. No matter how flawed it all is, it is a daily gift!

Your heart that beats, water from the tap, a blanket to keep you warm, a friend who cares, computers, wedding rings, dishwashing detergent, ceiling fans ... the list of things to be grateful for goes on and on endlessly.

This is all about how you think. Do you think joyful thoughts or do you immediately remind yourself of all the rottenness you have to deal with? At age fifteen, Jennifer Rothschild went blind from a rare condition. She could have woken up each day, dreading the daunting tasks ahead of her and wishing her life were easier. Instead, she wrote this in her book *Self Talk, Soul Talk*:

> During the writing of this book, I awoke one morning to a mountain of issues, and the first coherent thought I breathed into my pillow was *Ugh ... I am so stressed. I am so overwhelmed, I can't even face this day ... it's just too much....* In that predawn fuzziness, however ... something wonderful happened. It was as though a clarion light shot out of my thought closet to illuminate my self talk and bring clarity to the words I spoke to my soul. I began to say, *You are sufficient. You are present. You are here with me. And I can do all things through You who strengthens me!* ... I was speaking to my heavenly Father.[5]

Her thoughts were taken captive by a spirit of trust and gratitude for what she had been given. And we can do the same thing.

We are wired to forget to be grateful for the things we see every day. Those things become ordinary and not very exciting. It's exciting at first—the bigger apartment and the cute new husband and the new baby. But it all quickly becomes normal and ho-hum if we let it. Worse than that, often it actually becomes a burden. We have to guard against that mind-set with joy.

You don't have to wait for something exciting to happen to find joy. It's right within your hands! Make a decision right now about tomorrow. Instead of barely rolling out of bed after hitting the snooze button twice, decide you will get up with a new determination. Choose your favorite praise song and set it as your phone alarm. Commit now that no matter how you feel, you will get up at your chosen time.

It won't be easy, but you are worth the extra effort!

If you're not a morning person, then set your wake-up time appropriately. Don't try to push too hard against your habits until you get used to it. Ease into this, or you will burn out too quickly and set yourself up for defeat. Don't expect yourself to be bouncy and energetic, but still you can be thankful for the new day. Don't use your tendency to need coffee before you can talk to anyone as an excuse. You can still be joyful before your first cup. (I'm ducking from people throwing empty coffee mugs at me.)

I am the opposite. I am a morning person. I have a harder time being joyful at the end of the day. I'm tired, I get cranky, and the day I had so much hope for is over with at least a few disappointments. By about eight-thirty I want to climb into bed, watch a crime drama, and just hope for a better tomorrow.

So I have to choose to find the good in my evenings. I can play a table game with some of the kids or have a long talk with a teen. I can give some of that time to my husband and work on keeping our marriage strong. I could even park myself on the couch and let everyone come to me. It doesn't matter if I am tired; I just need to plug myself into the good that is all around me instead of letting the shadow of night overtake me.

> This day is holy to our Lord. Do not grieve, for the
> joy of the LORD is your strength. (Neh. 8:10)

SURRENDER YOUR IMAGINATION

Before I go on, please know that I am not perfect at any of this. I struggle and fail and have to pull myself out of the pit just like you. I don't write these principles from a place of mastering them. I write them from as deep a place of need as you have.

I have to capture those thoughts that I am too tired, too grumpy, too worn out to enjoy my family. Our minds can play tricks on us, and like I said at the beginning of this chapter, I make purposeful decisions about how I behave.

My dear friend Sheri Yates is one of the most incredible women I have ever known. She understands the glory of God in a way that inspires me. In her book *Stuck*, she calls it "surrendering your imagination" based on 2 Corinthians 10:5, which says, "We demolish arguments and every pretension that sets itself up against the knowledge of God, and we take captive every thought to make it obedient to Christ." She wrote, "Because I keep my mind on what God did today, yesterday, and every day, it captures my runaway mind so that my imagination aligns with God's dreams for me. We must reject any thought that disagrees with God's Word and continue to replace the trash with Truth!"[6]

My friends, the joy of the Spirit is yours for the asking! Grab it! Embrace it! Hold on to it with the same passion that you had for your dreams when you were a girl. There is more fulfillment in that kind of gift than anything you ever imagined!

As I stood there on that Saturday, feeling hurt that my kids were going to be spending the day outside, James walked across the yard to me and said, "Honey, they are fine. I am watching them. Go inside and do whatever you wanted to do."

He escorted me back into the house, and as he left, he clicked the lock on the knob and closed it behind him. I heard him tell the kids not to knock on the door but to get him if they needed something.

I felt stung by the guilt that I was rejecting my children. I didn't want them to feel "locked away" from me. I begged God for wisdom in what to do. I knew that, while it wasn't what I would have done, my children would be fine. Men see the needs of children differently than women do, but that doesn't make it wrong.

I finally decided to allow myself to finish cleaning the floor and then make the decision if I should let the children back in the house. I scrubbed the floors to my heart's content and enjoyed my praise music. Afterward, I peeked out the window to the backyard and saw that the kids were having their picnic. They all seemed to be enjoying themselves, so I decided to go ahead and give my bathroom a good scrubbing. After that, I went through all of the baby clothes and washed them. I kept peeking at the kids and then going back to my work, eventually letting God and my husband have the control I so desperately needed to let go of.

Around three o'clock I lay down for a nap. I felt James gently shaking me awake after what felt like fifteen minutes, but in reality had been three hours! It was six o'clock, the kids were back inside, and they all wanted to invite me to join them for pizza.

I rubbed the sleep from my eyes and staggered into the dining room, where my incredibly dirty, stinky children were laughing and enjoying a night of pizza and soda (not something we did very often) without plates. They just ate right off of napkins on the table as they talked about their day and shared with me all their adventures. They told me how they played pirates and made stick houses and how Daddy took them to the "fun store" (which turned out to be the local gas station/minimart) and let them each pick out an ice cream treat.

I sat there staring at their beaming little faces and thinking about how grateful I was that I had just let the day happen instead of allowing my frustration to put a stop to it all. They had fun, and my husband really appreciated that I trusted him instead of protesting his efforts. And the kids asked if they could do the whole thing again the next Saturday.

It didn't take much to talk me into it!

The next time (possibly five minutes from now) you are faced with your go-to negative reaction to a difficult moment, stop. Breathe. Take in something good. Ignore your hurting heart or your disappointment, and accept that you can make this into a beautiful experience. You can slow it down, think of something good, consider how you are coming across to the person you are talking to (kids, husband), and alter your reaction to fit the kind of woman you want to be. Ask God. Cry out to Him, "Father! Pour Your joy down on me, please!"

And He will.

Your simple assignment:

1. Below your three columns with the lines connecting them, draw a horizontal line, and in that space write three things you are grateful for in your problems.

2. Now draw hearts and doodles around those three things. (Don't skip this ... it just might surprise you!)

3. Write the word *joy* on a few sticky notes and hang them where you will see them often.

4. Read Nehemiah 8:9–12.

DO-OVER LIST

GIFTS	DREAMS	PROBLEMS
decorating	write a book	_boys' messy room_
frugal	_nice home_	unreliable car
photos	serve others	
hospitality	debt free	broken friendships

GRATITUDE

happy children

sewing machine

Christ

health

loving husband

a home

friends

nice weather

THERE'S JOY IN THE JOURNEY!

CHAPTER 8

Practice

I have never been one of those moms who wants her kids helping in the kitchen. My friends would tell me how their little darlings stood on a stool next to them while they baked cookies or pies, and I would think, *How do you get the baking done like that?!*

So maybe I have priority issues.

Or maybe I am a divide-and-conquer kind of girl who recognizes her weaknesses. I like spending time with my kids. I don't mind cooking. But doing them both at the same time, no. That, in my world, is a recipe for disaster.

So when the kids were all little and I set out to prepare a meal (which I had to do several times a day, of course), I would settle them into an activity at the table while I worked. I kept special art supplies and building toys tucked away in shoe boxes in a high cabinet so that when I pulled those boxes out and poured their contents onto the dining table, I could tell the kids to stay there and they would do it. The new toys or art materials were exciting enough to keep them occupied for at least fifteen minutes. Then I could use that time for all it was worth ... chop, boil, mix, and flip like a samurai at a Japanese steakhouse. It was hurry, hurry before they got tired of their activity.

One late afternoon the kids were all playing at the table, and I was putting together a simple spaghetti dinner when my four-year-old son decided he really didn't want to stay at the table this time. He had been especially needy that day, feeling a little bit sick, and he begged to stay by me while I cooked. I told him he could be in the kitchen with me *if* he sat still and just watched.

He is a very sweet and helpful boy and loves to have his hands into everything, so he couldn't resist trying to help by dumping the spaghetti out of the bag for me (all over the floor), bringing me various items from the pantry (none of which I needed to make spaghetti), and standing right next to me, leaning on my leg (with me constantly stepping on him).

By the time dinner was ready, I needed a vacation. Alone. To Paris.

AN IMAGINARY SWORD

We moms have so many teeny, tiny, insignificant responsibilities that pull us in different directions all day long that we can struggle to find a balance between what we need to do, what we want to do, and what we have to do. We need to check the diaper, answer the phone, solve a math problem, wipe up a spill, and pay the electric bill all in the same moment. We choose one and then the next, all the while pushing forward and hoping we're being wise. Minute by minute, day in and day out. Shuffle, step, shuffle.

I have talked in previous chapters about the problems you are having and the plans you will make to get past them, but when the time comes to implement those plans it is *one moment at a time*.

You don't win a war in one giant blast. You have a small battle, win or lose, keep going, prepare for the next, get better at it, and try again, until you look back upon more victories than losses and realize how far you have come.

You made your columns and lists. You put some ideas together and asked for inspiration. You have a battle plan. You know your strengths and have prayed for joy in any circumstance. Now you grab your imaginary sword of dreams and believe that you can do it, and into the day you go. Today. Let's take it one minute at a time.

Looking at each step in your day as an opportunity for victory means you can let go of the previous minute. It's gone. You messed up or you rejoiced or you settled for less than you should have, but in every case the moment is gone. This one is right here and you can change it. You aren't stuck in what you were doing five minutes ago. Just move forward.

If you yelled at your kids or tore down your husband or ripped the seam out—for the third time—on the dress you are making, you have the opportunity right now to turn that around and get a fresh start. You can still ask for forgiveness, build your husband back up, and start that seam one more time.

When you're having a really hard day, the kind they feature in laundry detergent commercials (you know, bloody stains and torn, mud-covered pants), you can still grab the moment you are in right now and flip it.

This is your do-over.

You are walking out the door on your way to an appointment, and you're running late. The dog, who technically belongs to your son even though he never takes care of it, rushes past you like a maniac as you open the gate, and he is gone. Great. Now you have to sprint down the street with your hair all fixed and non-running shoes on to find the dumb dog you would rather not have in the first place.

It feels like a terrible, out-of-control moment. Anger starts to swell within you. But wait. Breathe. Stop and slowly count to five. Let your mind settle into this new situation that you have been forced into. Don't answer the kids' questions for a few minutes; don't even tell them to be quiet. Just close your eyes and slow down.

Okay, you will be late. You are going to inconvenience people. You will not be helping your reputation of always being late, but it's done now. Move on. You aren't dressed for dog chasing. Okay. You can go back inside and grab your running shoes, or you can just face the hurt feet you will have if you chase the dog in the shoes you're wearing. There are more options, more decisions. You do the best you can with what you have in the moment.

What I am going to say next may seem odd, but stay with me.

You can actually have fun. After you take that breath and five-second thought, ask God to show you what it is in this moment that you can delight in. Running is good for you, your husband loves that dog, the kids will get some energy out, and you might meet a neighbor or a stranger who stops to help. Maybe just the sight of you crazily running down the street in your nice clothes followed by a four-year-old would cheer up your housebound neighbor. Maybe God caused all of this for her pleasure.

And even if none of that happens, you can create the fun your-self. There is something you can do with this that no one else can do in exactly the same way you can. I can give you tips, and I will, but the deepest joy will come from bringing your own special touch.

THE EASY BUTTON

Other writers have shared this same principle of your uniqueness in their own beautiful ways. In *A Million Little Ways*, Emily P. Freeman says,

> Could it also be that there are things in you that aren't in anyone else? That the way God has attached himself to you is a unique way he wants to display his glory to the world? Do you believe in his power to bring life out of death? Could it also be possible, then, that he can bring life out of you? Could there be some corner of the room he wants to influence and you are the person he has called to do that? It may not look like what you expect it to look like or the way other people expect it to look. You were made in the secret place, woven together on purpose with threads made from sacred longings that come not only from you but from the heart of God—he wove you together with a personality and you bring your own you-ness to the table.[1]

If you are dedicated to letting the Holy Spirit rain joy upon you, then you can take that joy a step further and turn even the most frustrating moments into a good time. You still have your problems. You are still working with your plan. You are still using your talents. You are just going to stop for a minute and look for a way to catch the breath of right now and reset. It's almost as simple as pushing a button.

Remember that Easy Button that was so popular a few years ago? It was appealing, wasn't it? The concept was from a Staples ad that showed it making life easier. Later it became an actual product that you could set on your desk to press when you got in a jam. Instant stress relief. Bam.

Well, we don't need a big red button to get stress relief. God built it right into us, and if we will slow down long enough to realize it, we'll see we have it anytime we need.

FIVE STEPS

Here is a five-step formula to get you started with flipping those irritating situations into something that will create a joy-filled memory.

1. Breathe deeply.

2. Pray and praise.

3. Dig through your bag of tricks.

4. Take a step of faith.

5. Repeat if necessary.

Breathe Deeply

I have already mentioned this several times in previous chapters. Take a breath. Breathing is instinctive. Twelve to twenty times per minute, your lungs expand and contract, taking in oxygen and pushing out carbon dioxide. Your heart sends the oxygen to the cells of your tissues and organs. Studies have shown time and again that deep breathing and slow release calms you and creates a healthy environment for your body in many, many ways. Take a long breath in through your nose and listen to the sound of the air going in. Hold it for a few seconds, then release it slowly.

When I am really in need of de-stressing, I also slowly raise my arms over my head while I take my breath. This opens up my lungs and helps me focus on slow arm movements, which controls my air intake. As I breathe out, I let my arms down slowly. You may feel in a panic, but you have time for this. You need it.

Pray and Praise

I've said it before and will say it again and again and again. Prayer changes you, changes your situation, changes your focus, and centers you in the middle of a frantic day.

So as you breathe out, call upon the name of Christ. You don't need to be eloquent. Just say whatever comes to your mind. Often I will just say His name over and over again. "Jesus. Jesus. Jesus."

As I was writing this book, a friend offered me her beach cottage so I could have a quiet place to write as my deadline loomed. On the last morning, I knew I needed to get more done than seemed humanly possible, and I wanted to jump right in. I felt a sense of urgency because I knew that when I went back home, as hard as I might try, I would not be able to focus the way I could at her cottage.

My mind raced as I sat down to try to write. I felt a panic as nothing came and my fingers stood still over the keyboard. No! I prayed, "God, I need to finish this!" Then I remembered, breathe. Slow down. I knew I would make better use of my limited time if I took fifteen minutes making myself slow down than if I jumped out of the starting gate early.

I stood up from my computer and, still in my pajamas, walked down to the end of the pier across the road from the cottage and sat. I stared out at the ocean and breathed in the calm of the water. I let my mind empty of what I wanted to do and say in my book and let the Holy Spirit fill me with His presence. Deep breath. Deep prayer. Deep quiet. After about ten minutes I started to whisper a song of praise. It wasn't a song or tune I had heard before. Just words that came to mind as I focused more on Him and less on me, set to a mysterious melody. "Magnificent—worthy—wonderful—holy—beautiful—all-knowing ..." in a simple tune that was forgotten as quickly as it came out of my mouth. It didn't matter. Only He could hear me.

After only fifteen minutes, I walked back to the cottage and sat down to type. The words rushed through me. The oxygen to my lungs had opened my mind, and the life-giving power of prayer and praise had opened my soul.

Never underestimate the difference even the shortest prayer and simplest praise can make.

Dig Through Your Bag of Tricks

Remember Felix the Cat? (If you're too young to remember, google him ... he's awesome!) He carries around a yellow bag, his Bag of

Tricks, that is filled with whatever he needs when he gets in a pinch. I remember as a kid being amazed that he could pull an escalator or an airplane out of his bag!

His theme song starts with, "Felix the Cat, the wonderful, wonderful cat. Whenever he gets in a fix, he reaches into his bag of tricks."

Felix has enemies all around who try to steal the bag, but he always gets the last laugh. Only he can really get anything useful from the magic bag. The enemies just end up getting hurt.

You have a bag of tricks too, but they can't be stolen from you. They are all yours to use whenever you need them. Even when it seems all is lost, like you can't find a way to pull it out of yourself, you can still use those gifts God gave you.

You have your list; now use it. You have your suitcase filled with fruits of the Spirit, so pull some of those out! Clear your mind of what you want to happen, and wrap your brain around what is actually happening. Then think of ways, using your own uniqueness, to flip it from miserable to pleasing.

Joni Eareckson Tada, despite being a paraplegic, loves to paint. She could see the art in her mind and needed only to find a way to express it without the use of her arms to help her. She figured out how—and this constantly amazes me—to paint with the brush between her teeth. In one of her YouTube videos, she shares that her art is an expression of things that are uniquely her. Then she puts it out there for the encouragement of others and for God's glory. Incredible!

Your talents are there for you to pull out of your bag. Singing, painting, cooking, building, catching a ball, calming an animal ... keep adding to your list. Then there are your deeper talents—encouraging, teaching, serving, showing mercy. They're all there for you to draw from when you need help.

> We have different gifts, according to the grace given to each of us. If your gift is prophesying, then prophesy in accordance with your faith; if it is serving, then serve; if it is teaching, then teach; if it is to encourage, then give encouragement; if it is giving, then give generously; if it is to lead, do it diligently; if it is to show mercy, do it cheerfully. (Rom. 12:6–8)

Then when those single, simple moments of difficulty sneak up on you, use your talents. Your art can be more than paint and paper. If you can see how to draw a still life, then you can pull that out of your bag when you're facing a hard moment. Instead of drawing on paper, draw on the artistic qualities of the things around you.

When the dog runs away, look at the world like only an artist can. See the dog's legs pumping as a thing of beauty and embrace the wonder of it. As you search for him, notice the curves of the road and the neighbor's well-manicured lawn. The colors and movement and shadows are something only you would notice. Point them out to your kids, and encourage them to pick out one thing about this experience of chasing the dog down the street to tell Daddy about later. Maybe even have them draw what they thought was fun or fascinating that afternoon when you are home and trying to settle them so you can do a task. Use this experience to find your inner dreamer and laugh.

Or if you're a chef, think of ways to mix the ingredients of this situation and come out with something better and delicious (just don't cook the dog). You may even find ways to write it into a "recipe for taking care of a dog" and give that to your son to carry out.

Of course, you still have to do the work of finding the dog, luring him to you, locking him up, and later brainstorming ways to prevent this from happening again. Enjoying a moment does not mean we have to want to do it again. We're not crazy.

Take a Step of Faith

Step—no, leap—into the enjoyment. If you're chasing a dog, see the ridiculousness and embrace it. It is funny. If you're rolling the toilet paper back on the roll for the tenth time this week because your two-year-old can't seem to end her curiosity about this spinning roll of wonder, dig into your bag and do something different than what you have been doing. Instead of rolling it back on the roll, stuff it into a Mason jar, set it on the floor by the potty, and call it a creative toilet paper dispenser.

Be bold and see your available responses to your problems as unique and crazy and who-cares-if-it-is-weird. The very best moments in your life won't be an imitation of what someone else has done. They will be filled with what only you can bring to the occasion.

When I sang my whisper song to God, I wasn't looking for His approval. I was declaring His greatness. I was setting aside my own weakness and being filled with His glory. My trust in Him freed me to let out the song that only I could write. I'm no songwriter; I have no talent for that. I'm a decorator. So I saw the illumination of the sun reflecting on the ocean. I noticed the texture of the slight ripples. I sang of the beauty of the lone bird barely skimming the water in a hundred-yard-long swoop as he ever so lightly brushed along the surface. I saw God's hand in the workmanship, and I made my song about that. I stepped out with my own uniqueness and used it to praise Him for the beauty of my life.

Lysa TerKeurst explains it like this:

> Oh, how powerful it is to shift from an attitude to gratitude and to praise our God in the midst of it all. When I do this, my circumstances may not instantly change, but the way I look at those circumstances certainly does. I stop being blind to all that's right and see so many more reasons to praise God. And when my heart is full of praise, my emotions aren't nearly as prone to coming unglued![2]

YOUR OWN SPECIAL LENS

When you are having a hard moment, look at it through your own special lens. The one you can find only after you have let the oxygen flow through your body, released the carbon dioxide, and then prayed a prayer that is intimately between you and God. There's no one to impress here. It's just you. You need to have these times with Him so you can get at least a tiny glimpse of the truth of your problems: that they are safely in the hand of a loving Father and that He will lead you through to a better tomorrow, even if you are the only thing better about it.

By risking being fully yourself and attacking your crisis moments with your own sense of style and flair, you are daring to believe you can overcome this. Even if nothing else changes—if the dog doesn't come back and the ladies at your appointment get angry for your lateness, among the many other consequences you will have to face from the unexpected direction this moment has taken—you can enjoy it!

It doesn't mean you don't care that you created problems for others or that you are irreverent about it. You can apologize and be humble and still be joyful.

You can unwrap the memory like a gift that will carry you through the rest of the day. Something to laugh about at the dinner table. Something to learn from as you carry on through the future. You have seen that you have attitudes you need to adjust and there are people you need to learn to work with despite their own difficulty in handling hard moments. The struggles are a gift of growth and life and expression of something great in you that God wants to show you how to use.

> Consider it pure joy, my brothers and sisters, whenever you face trials of many kinds, because you know that the testing of your faith produces perseverance. Let perseverance finish its work so that you may be mature and complete, not lacking anything. (James 1:2–4)

C-A-T

After our disastrous spaghetti dinner preparations, my son continued to be sick into the next day. I canceled all of my planned activities and just sat with him. The other kids played around us as we snuggled on the couch and I read to him his favorite book, *The Cat in the Hat,* over and over.

I hoped all of our reading and snuggling would satisfy him as I slipped away at five thirty to make dinner. Nope. He was onto me. He wrapped himself in his blanket and shuffled into the kitchen and again asked if he could stay with me.

Ugh.

Okay.

This time, even though I was tired and he was fussier than the day before, I decided to ask for God's help. It was a detail I had forgotten to do the night before. He showed me that I could find a way to turn it into a fun experience for us both. I dug into my bag of tricks and mentally searched for a way to help us both with our mutual problem ... how to make dinner with a sick boy needing his mama.

One of my gifts and dreams is teaching. It comes in handy on occasion in my daily life, so I hooked on to that idea. How could I use my natural gift of teaching to occupy a grumpy little boy while I cooked dinner, allowing him to be content with staying near me but give me room to get my cooking done?

I was making our standard fallback dinner that I always cook when it's been a rough day: breakfast. Biscuits, eggs, and fruit. My routine was to mix, knead, and roll out the biscuits, then pop them into the oven. While they baked I could cut up some fruit to make a fruit salad (the best way to stretch a small amount of fruit for a large family) and scramble the eggs. Since it was dinner I could add a bit of cheese to the eggs. (I told you that's all I know.)

I let him follow me around as I got out the ingredients for the biscuits (he was too big for me to hold) and enlisted his "help" in carrying the salt to the counter. I talked about the book we had read earlier and added some of my own story elements to keep his attention. Then, as I prepared to begin the part of the meal preparation that required more focus, I set him on the counter near where I was mixing the dry ingredients for the biscuits. I pulled a nine-by-thirteen-inch baking pan out from the cabinet and poured two cups of flour into it, using a measuring cup and counting out loud as if the amount of flour that went into the pan was important. "One, two," I said as I poured another cup into the cake pan. "There, this is yours," and I slid the pan of flour over to him. I then carefully measured two teaspoons of salt (no reason, I was just making it up) and let him pour each teaspoon into the flour. I handed him a spoon to stir his own mix together as I stirred my bowl of ingredients into biscuit dough.

I told him that his was not for dinner but for the story we were telling. I shook the pan and let the flour settle into a clean, shallow layer. "Now"—I smiled at him as I kneaded the biscuit dough—"you can make letters in the pan." I took my finger and started a word: c-a- … "I'm writing *cat*. You finish it." He rubbed his little hand in the pan and etched a childlike *t* into the flour. Then we shook it out and made another word. Then another.

He loved the game and loved playing with the flour. I kept his attention by talking about the story and making it more interesting by adding our own imagination to it. "What if the cat had been caught by the children's mother? What would she have done?" I crazily scratched my fingers in his flour pan as if I were the angry mother, which made him laugh. We thought of new story ideas and continued to draw letters and words into the flour.

By the time dinner was at the table, all the kids wanted to know more about this new game. The "flour game," they called it. They were delighted with the idea of making up their own endings to familiar stories and the thought of playing with a pan filled with flour.

I had turned what I had expected to be a miserable task into something fun, and as an added bonus we came up with a game that we used for years whenever one of the kids needed some special attention.

What kind of flour game is in your bag?

Your simple assignment:

1. On the back of your chart, write one of the problems you had yesterday. It can be anything, no matter how small (maybe one that you generally wouldn't tell someone about). Then pray for guidance in that area.

2. Below the problem, write down three things you could have done to add joy to that—just you on your own, not what anyone else could have done.

3. Circle one of those things that you will apply to the next little problem you have.

4. Read 1 Corinthians 9:24–27.

CHAPTER 9

Motherhood

Grocery shopping is my nemesis. I despise doing it. Something always goes wrong. I always forget something important. And it has to be done at least once a week. Dread.

Before my children were old enough to stay home alone, I would time my shopping trips during the store's least busy hours so it would be as empty of customers as possible. Sometimes that meant going shopping at five in the morning, but it was worth it. Wrangling a bunch of kids and a shopping cart while trying to find everything you need and stick to a budget is my idea of a living nightmare.

I remember having a baby carrier hooked on to the seat of the cart, one child in the basket area meant for holding your purchases, and five more kids walking along behind me, lined up in order of age, oldest in the back. I knew there was no point in trying to rush, despite my desperation to finish and go home, where I didn't have to check behind me every three seconds to be sure a kid hadn't either run off or been nabbed (there had been a string of child abductions in grocery stores in the nineties that led to my paranoia). I do learn from my mistakes, and I knew that rushing only made the whole experience worse.

I would go slowly down each aisle, pausing to move the children out of the way of other shoppers as much as possible, then ease back into the flow of traffic, filling my cart and hoping I didn't forget something at the back of the store. I needed to be as efficient as possible. No retracing my steps.

I would always add a box of Goldfish crackers to the cart, letting the children know they would be allowed to eat them as soon as we got into the van if they would just behave well so we could get through this experience.

Once home, there was the task of unloading the Goldfish crumb–covered children from the van and then carrying all of the groceries into the house and putting them away. Gee, it sounds so easy when I type it. But just the memory of it sends me into flashbacks that cause me to slightly understand what soldiers go through when they come home from war.

I would try to make it home just before lunch so I could stick the kids at the table with whatever was left of the crackers and some slices of cheese while I put everything in its proper place. Then, if all the stars aligned, the younger ones would go down for their naps at the same time, and I would have a glorious hour all to myself. #fantasyland

I remember vividly one day after getting home from an outing that went a little wilder than usual. For some reason I never understood, the kids were more energetic than their normal state of too much energy, which is saying a lot. And while you want your kids to get along, you don't want them conspiring against you and hyping each other up. This day, that is exactly what happened. One would start to cause trouble, and just as I turned to deal with it another one would dash off behind me and create a new mess. I felt like I was trying to round up a cageful of monkeys ... without a cage!

That's when I got the idea. If they were going to act like wild animals, then I would take advantage of that. "STOP!" I said firmly. "Everybody freeze!" I froze in my place in a contorted position. They weren't sure what to do, but the older ones stood completely still and the little ones got quiet. "Okay, here's what we are gonna do," I called out. "This is a zoo. And you are the monkeys. Ready. Set. Go!" I began to whoop around the kitchen like a baboon on caffeine. I did my best monkey sounds and ape walk, scratching myself under my arms, swaying back and forth while dragging my feet.

The kids were shocked. Stunned to the point of freezing right where they stood. Next I called out another animal—"Let's be lions!"—and I went into lion mode. They started to join in the game. I called out their names one at a time followed by an animal: "You are a snake!" and "You be a duck!" (I didn't worry that these animals would never be together in one place for real.) The kids and I spent the next five minutes playing "zoo," and I ended it with them being sharks having a feeding frenzy on the table (Goldfish, of course! What else would sharks eat?).

I had officially made my own reset. I pushed the button and changed what was happening. I didn't yell or get frustrated or wish my life was different. I just deflected their energy and gave us all a fresh new start. Plus, I thought it was fun too!

New starts are naturally built into our day. They happen organically all around us: the sun rises, our hearts beat, the kids laugh, lights turn on, the car starts, paychecks are deposited, clean clothes are worn—the list goes on forever. We also create new starts without thinking about it by making coffee, emptying the dishwasher, making the bed, changing a diaper, starting a book, taking out trash, checking the mailbox, or calling a friend.

THE BEST MEDICINE

Now I want us to take that all a step further by giving ourselves a fresh start on purpose. Pushing the button, so to speak. We can take our problems and all of that joy we have found and use it to change our lives and the lives of our families in ways that will rock our world, from the inside. And we will add one more element to the problem-solving puzzle ... humor.

When Abraham and Sarah found out they were expecting a baby when he was one hundred and she was ninety, they laughed a *lot*. Abraham fell on his face with laughter, and after the baby was born Sarah said, "God has brought me laughter, and everyone who hears about this will laugh with me" (Gen. 21:6).

Most of us can remember desperately wanting to have a baby. I did. We were married four years before our oldest daughter was born, and I had begun to believe I may be unable to bear children. I was heartbroken. Each month I hoped, and my hopes were dashed when my cycle started. But as much as I wanted to be a mother, I don't know if I would have started laughing if I had a baby when I was ninety! My last baby was born when I was forty-two, and the thing you heard me doing was crying out, "Oh, my aching back!"

Sarah not only laughed, but she also seemed to delight in knowing that everyone who heard would laugh too. Laughter is contagious, and when people see us finding humor in what looks like a very difficult situation, it can turn their days into joy as well.

We are affecting the people around us in some way. Let it be with joy and humor!

In *Cold Tangerines*, Shauna Niequist calls it celebration:

> Celebration when you think you're calling the shots? Easy. Celebration when your plan is working? Anyone can do that. But when you realize that the story of your life could be told a thousand different ways, that you could tell it over and over as a tragedy, but you choose to call it an epic, that's when you start to learn what celebration is. When what you see in front of you is so far outside of what you dreamed, but you have the belief, the boldness, the courage to call it beautiful instead of calling it wrong, that's celebration.[1]

You are likely thinking, *Easy for you to say, Lisa. You're not sitting here with my problems. I haven't had a shower for three days, and I can't even find my phone to place a call for help.* Right. It is hard. If it were easy, it wouldn't have any real value.

True peace and true joy and real contentment actually take effort and a willingness to step back and look at your situation as an opportunity instead of a burden. That's why most people never find it. They won't look in the right places.

I had no concept of this as a younger woman. I thought happiness meant comfort and ease. I thought pleasure was my goal and anything less was something I needed to get rid of. Sure, I prayed. I asked God to take away all of my problems and make me comfortable.

Then I became a mother, and I saw that my baby wanted the same thing ... to never be uncomfortable. But there were times when I knew that the discomfort was good for her. My baby never liked baths, but she needed to get clean to stay healthy. She would protest going to sleep even though I knew she was exhausted. She refused to let anyone but Mommy hold her, even though I occasionally needed to put her in someone else's arms where I knew she was perfectly safe and loved.

She couldn't be comfortable all the time. And then the lightbulb lit up over my head. Duh! Maybe the same was true for me! Maybe seeking comfort was the wrong thing to live for! Lisa, meet wisdom. You two should really get to know each other.

I dug into Scripture and found truth: that my goal should be to enjoy my life no matter what is happening to me. I don't need to look for discomfort, of course. It finds me every day. But I need to *decide* to be joyful and peaceful and Spirit filled in my situation while I work my way out of it. And motherhood is the perfect opportunity to put that into practice.

A MESSY LIFE

Even though we love being moms and wouldn't give it up for all the tea in China, it has challenges we were not prepared for. Other people's babies are so adorable, and before we had kids, when we heard moms complaining about how hard it is, we thought we knew what they meant. We criticized moms at the mall who were scream-ing at their children as the kids tried desperately to run away from them.

Then we became them.

I'm not a screamer, but I have other unpleasant reactions when my kids interrupt my momentum. I huff and slump and let them know they are a problem for me. It's awful. At the end of the day when I look back on all of my missed opportunities to build up my children, I grieve. And feel guilty. Guilt is the enemy of motherhood.

But we can turn that around! Let's start with knowing that we absolutely will fail our kids. No way around that. No human is capable of perfectly raising another human being. It's positively, 100 percent IM-possible. God was the only perfect parent, and even His children messed up. Your friend who looks like she has the per-fect life? It's not true. And if you are trying to look like you have the perfect life, stop. You're not helping anyone, especially your kids, by trying to appear flawless.

What we need to do is relax. Relax our idea that things should look a certain way or that our neighbor is doing a better job than we are or that kids should never mess up in our home. Messes are GOOD. Messes are LIFE! Messes are what make us LEARN!

Now, I like clean. I like tidy. I think better when my area is straight and my day is going smoothly. But when that flows over into being uptight about the messes and critical of my children's imperfections, it is harmful. It's harmful to me and to my family. It is time we find a balance between what we want our life to look like and what it *can* look like.

In my world, I found a middle place between clean and messy. We have a pick-up time every day before dinner. All day long people can use the house, make a mess, spread their Legos out on the table (never the floor ... NO LEGOS ON THE FLOOR!), and create, build, explore. Then, before dinner we clean it all up. It's all tidy for Mommy and ready for a clean start to the next day. I have a small area where they can keep their messes out if they are in the middle of a project, but the rest has to go back to its place where it belongs.

So all day long, as the messiness feels like it is taking over, I choose to see the fun and humor of each situation. The boys taking apart broken appliances; that is fun. They are learning so much and really get excited over teeny bits of metal and wire. The girls making jewelry on the kitchen table with beads rolling across the floor; what's not fun about that? Sure, it's a mess that will likely leave its mark for years as I find beads in odd places every time I sweep, but their creativity is lighting something inside of them on fire.

Those are the good messes, but what about the less pleasant ones? The throw-up, the broken lamp, the poop smeared all over the side of the toilet. They are just as much a part of your life as beads and Legos, so let's choose to enjoy them too! I know it's poop ... I am not insane. I don't love it. And I will teach that child not to do that again, but come on ... it's funny.

Grab the rag, the cleaning spray, and the criminal mastermind who managed to create poop art without you noticing and head into the bathroom. You can show him that you love to spend time together even when the task is unpleasant. Sit while you make him clean it up (yes, of course you'll sneak back in later and really clean it) and talk to him. Forget that your friend is waiting for you to return her call and enjoy this moment with your son. Then show him how to properly wash his hands with enthusiasm. Make it fun for him. You don't have to be disapproving for him to learn his lesson. You can enjoy the time together despite the unpleasantness of the situation.

If he does it again, it becomes a new problem, and you make a new plan like we talked about before. One step at a time. This too shall pass.

My friend Lysa (we are friends in my mind) makes this adorable point in her book *Unglued*:

> So, in the midst of an unglued moment, how do I shift from *having an attitude* to *walking in gratitude*? I need a go-to script that will redirect my perspective to a better place. And I think I have just the thing. I say out loud to myself, "If this is the worst thing that happens to me today, it's still a pretty good day.[2]

When the day gets rough, take a breath, follow the outline in chapter 8, and relax. It really is not as big as it seems. Our grip on truth slips a little when the unexpected happens and we immediately grab the notion that what is happening is bad. Usually it is simply a side step to our plans. Instead of walking straight to the van when it's time to leave the house like we want to, we are forced to take a separate route. That might include taking a three-year-old to the bathroom (after she's already been buckled in), forgetting the plate of cookies we were supposed to take with us (so back into the house again), and then once more back inside to look for the pacifier. Getting into the van may not look like you thought it should, but that doesn't mean it's wrong. It can be filled with joy.

Why not skip back to the house the second time you have to go in for the cookies? How about tickling your child as she climbs back in after going potty? "The tickle monster visits girls who don't go potty before they get in the van," you might say as you buckle her up. There are many, many ways to add joy and humor to an unplanned side step, and those ways can be uniquely yours.

Sometimes the problems are bigger than potty issues. Illness, death, financial crisis, broken relationships, and depression can all wreak havoc if we aren't careful. While these things are complicated and often devastating, there is still joy in them. The flower bud that breaks through the cement and shows the glory of the Creator is inspiration that we can find something beautiful in any circumstance.

Motherhood is one of the great gifts of your life. It will grow you and stretch you and send you to your knees in desperation. And it is filled with opportunities for so much joy that we can't even comprehend the magnitude of it. In a million little ways it will change you. Will the changes be for the better or the worse? You decide. It's up to you.

I choose better. I want to breathe through the trials and look past the burden of the tantrums and flaws that my children have and see the blessing of learning together. I want to show my kids that their mom enjoyed her life no matter what was happening around her. I want them to witness me enjoying *them* no matter how they act or what they do. God enjoys me that way; I can pass that on to my kids.

> He brought me out into a spacious place; he res-
> cued me because he delighted in me. (Ps. 18:19)

MOM'S TOOL KIT

We need some tools to be able to build the kind of life where we respond to difficulty with delight and humor. So let's build ourselves a tool kit.

When I work on remodel projects, tools get easily lost. Especially when my husband is working with me. He puts down the tool he is using wherever he is when he is finished with it, and then when we need it two hours later, we can't find it. Drives me bananas.

So I got myself my own tools. I painted them pink and wrote "MOM" in Sharpie all over them. (There's a business idea ... mono-grammed pink tools for women that fit in the junk drawer in the kitchen.) Then I got a five-gallon bucket, which I also painted pink, and bought a "bucket apron" that ties around it and has pockets for every tool (someone had angels whispering in her ear when she invented this). I keep all of my pink tools neatly in my bucket. Then I got James a bucket too, located all of our other tools that we had been using, and gave that to him. "These are yours and those [point-ing to pinkie] are mine."

Whenever I start a new project I get out my pink apron tool bucket. I decide what tools I need and load them into each pocket, getting organized to start the remodel. I am armed and ready to tear out walls and install window coverings.

We can take that same principle and apply it to turning our hard moments around. I can make myself an arsenal of tools that will be ready for me to grab when I need them.

1. Strength

> Do you not know? Have you not heard? The LORD is the everlasting God, the Creator of the ends of the earth. He will not grow tired or weary, and his understanding no one can fathom. He gives strength to the weary and increases the power of the weak. Even youths grow tired and weary, and young men stumble and fall; but those who hope in the LORD will renew their strength. They will soar on wings like eagles; they will run and not grow weary, they will walk and not be faint. (Isa. 40:28–31)

2. Courage

> Be strong and take heart, all you who hope in the LORD. (Ps. 31:24)

Making these changes can be scary. But God is right there to fight for your victory!

3. Perseverance

> Therefore, since we have been justified through faith, we have peace with God through our Lord Jesus Christ, through whom we have gained

access by faith into this grace in which we now stand. And we boast in the hope of the glory of God. Not only so, but we also glory in our sufferings, because we know that suffering produces perseverance; perseverance, character; and character, hope. And hope does not put us to shame, because God's love has been poured out into our hearts through the Holy Spirit, who has been given to us. (Rom. 5:1–5)

I want these things: character, hope, and endurance. I just don't really want to go through what I have to in order to have them! But it's unavoidable. And better than that, getting through your difficulties with victory is a gift—not necessarily the problem itself, but the opportunity to see something good in it and learn through the discovery. Don't underestimate what you are learning from all of your struggles. It is what will make you wise and beautiful!

4. Salvation

And this is the testimony: God has given us eternal life, and this life is in his Son. Whoever has the Son has life; whoever does not have the Son of God does not have life. I write these things to you who believe in the name of the Son of God so that you may know that you have eternal life. (1 John 5:11–13)

If you don't yet know the joy of salvation, let me tell you, it is the ultimate do-over. You get forgiveness and a renewing of your mind like you have never imagined. Christ died for you … yes, you! He took the price that you should pay for your sins and paid it for you. He went to hell and came back, and now He not only stands at the right hand of the Father but also stands with you and helps you when you need anything. He is love; He is everything. I urge you to stop reading this book right now; set it down, and ask God to become your Lord and Savior. This will become the greatest tool in your arsenal.

If you already have this tool, *use* it! Your salvation is what gives you insight you couldn't have any other way. You now have a connection with God and have constant access to Him through the Holy Spirit. You are no longer separated from Him, and that, my precious friend, is what will give you the strength to find true joy, no matter what your circumstances are.

5. Truth

> Teach me your way, LORD, that I may rely on your
> faithfulness; give me an undivided heart, that I may
> fear your name. (Ps. 86:11)

It takes maturity to see that what we currently believe may not be true. We are a product of many things in the world. I am constantly realizing that something I have thought to be true all my life is wrong! We are all a work in process, but being willing to see truth and let go of old ideas is a sure way to move ahead toward joy.

The list is too long for any of us to name, but beware of what you automatically believe from childhood or what is being fed to you by the media. Do you know that you are more precious than silver? Do you know that God thinks you are worth dying for? It's the truth! And there's more where that came from.

These five things are a start. But there is much more you can put in your toolbox. Look at your situation and see what you need. Patience? Peace? Mercy? The tools at your disposal are countless.

When you think of a tool you need, find Bible verses to go with it, and make yourself a list. Keep it wherever works best for you. I like using my iPhone, but a written list with pen and paper works just as well. Then refer to that list every time you feel the need for that tool. It is amazing how much it will help you find all the humor and release that you need to get through the hard days.

Then add in the humor. It's okay if you laugh while quoting Scripture. It doesn't have to be all serious and stoic. God created laughter, and He loves it when we enjoy ourselves! If you don't find anything funny, then find the delight. Shout it out to Him in a spirit of rejoicing. Think of humor as the salt to a whole meal. It isn't the biggest ingredient, but it makes everything else taste better.

It looks like this: crisis moment … stop and breathe … think of verses that will help you find what you need (strength, patience, and so on) … pray … relax … laugh … reset activity (this will be covered more in chapter 10) … back to your day.

I know it sounds so easy, but it definitely is not. Especially at first. You are fighting your habits and your nature and reversing your usual responses. But I promise that in time (and not a long time either!) it will become a new habit and you will become a new creature.

AWKWARD LAUGHTER

In *Stuck*, Sheri Yates has this to add about creating habits of joy:

> If negativity creeps in your mind, cast it down and
> replace it with truth. For example, if you think, *I
> am stupid*, cast it down and contradict it, "No! I
> have the mind of Christ, and it doesn't matter if the
> world assumes I'm stupid." When you notice your
> negative attitude, sit down right away and write one
> hundred things you are thankful for. Remember
> the good things God has done in your life and the
> gifts He has blessed you with. Every time. If you do
> it enough, you will change. You will transform into
> a more positive person.[3]

Maybe it's just me, but I want to be a *new* creature! This old one is looking too much like the Loch Ness Monster most of the time.

So I laugh. I laugh when milk spills; I laugh when the credit card gets rejected; I laugh when I am running late.

I don't mean a guffaw, "Who cares?" kind of laughing. It's not "That lady has lost it" laughter. I am talking about a deep acceptance that there is not much I can do to change what is happening right now, so I may as well enjoy it and then resolve to make a plan to change it for tomorrow. It's relief. It's sunshine on a cloudy day (great, now I am stuck on that song).

It will feel awkward, laughing when you're in the middle of a crisis moment. I know. But try it, and you will see that it is very effective.

Just the act of smiling lifts your heart. Right now, while you are reading, smile really big and hold it for five seconds. Did it help? Did it change the way you feel just the teeniest bit? You can carry that into your bigger moments when you're not reading but are trying to deal with a rebellious five-year-old who refuses to do what you tell him.

You still have to work out a plan for teaching him to do what you say, but right now, in this moment, you can respond with joy anyway. However you decide to handle the situation, getting angry will only make it worse. So do your steps from chapter 8, smile, and then—and this is the fun part—do something unexpected.

You could start to hum a playful tune or march in place while pretending to beat a drum. Incorporate your child into it, and give him an imaginary instrument so he can join you. Play with him for a minute, then gently tell him that he needs to do what you say, and carry on.

It sounds like it will look crazy. It's definitely a fine line. But crazy is out of control, and you are being very in control. In fact, you are taking control of your responses, maybe for the first time, and deciding how this moment will look. You are shaking it up on purpose instead of being at the mercy of the world around you.

Another tool you will need is a plan for this unexpected activity. Yes, I know it sounds like I have twisted that ... planning *and* unexpected. But listen, in the moment when you need to switch your attitude and help the kids refocus, you might not be able to think of a fun activity. Having some ideas ahead of time takes the panic out and replaces it with fun.

When you're watching TV or going out to dinner with your husband or on the phone with a friend, jot down anything that comes to mind as a running list of fun, quick ideas of things to do when your day gets frazzled. Keep it in your phone with your Bible verse arsenal. Write down ideas like my zoo game. Be creative.

I know that's not easy, so I'll give you tons of ideas at the end of the book. But I want to show you here how to find your own crazy ideas. It's just anything that comes to mind as you look around, even if it's impossible. Is there a bush by your front door? Put "Climb the bush" on your list. Okay, the bush will get ruined if you tell your kids to climb it, but it's just a seed of an idea. It makes you aware of what is around you and will lead to some really fun activities down the line.

I once lived in an area where all the trees were pine trees. If you don't know, that means there were no branches for the first forty feet. No way can you climb that! But one day my kids really needed to get some energy out and those pine trees were all I had. There were five of them in my yard, so I found construction paper and nailed one color to each tree. I put a lawn chair in the middle of them and started yelling out colors. The kids had to run from one color to the next. I turned this activity into a game with rules and prizes. (The prizes don't have to be big; they could be that the winner gets to choose the colors on the trees next time or gets to choose everyone's clothes the next day.)

There is an endless number of possibilities, and your list will grow and change. So try to think of just a few to start with. Keep it tucked away and be prepared. It's so much easier to jump into a do-over when you have some ideas ready. Then when the time comes, you can alter the activity to fit the needs of the moment. If you're in the grocery store, for example, and you can't swing around like monkeys, change it to acting like animals while being completely silent. Maybe you have to guess which animal they are pretending to be. The kids will love it.

We have played versions of that zoo game many, many times over the years since I first did that. When the need arises, I call out, "Everybody freeze!" and we go into a surprise action. Farm games and Bible characters and acting out movies or just moving in slow motion for five minutes can really make a difference in how your day moves forward.

You will also need a list of ideas for when you need a personal do-over. Not every need will include the whole family. Sometimes Mama needs a do-over all by herself. Personally, I love crushed ice from Sonic. So I keep a bag of ice in my freezer, and when I need a moment to myself I make a glass of ice with sparkling water and a splash of essential oils and sit out on the front porch. I only need ten minutes, and then I can pick up where I left off. If the kids need supervision they can play around me, but I let them know this is "Mama time."

There's nothing wrong with having a moment to yourself. Susanna Wesley, mother of John and Charles Wesley, had ten children who survived, and she endured many hardships. Her dedication to prayer was strong, but it was difficult to find a place to pray. So she would flip her apron over her head, and the children knew not to bother her when she had that apron up.

If she can teach ten children to leave her alone for a few quiet moments, so can you! You can teach your children to wait for you; you can ignore the phone and emails for a short time; and you can let the dishes go for long enough to take a breath, turn your thoughts back to God, and find your joy.

CONNECTIONS

On that day in my kitchen when we played, I decided to enjoy my children. I let go of my agenda to finish my task, tapped into the energy they had, and made a game out of it. It plugged Mom into the excitement and let them know how much I delight in them.

While they were at the table eating their ocean feast, I kept talking to them as I put the groceries away. I told them to hold their breath while I counted to three or to pretend to be swimming by just using their arms (staying seated), and they kept being sharks for the whole meal. All I had to do was think of what a shark or fish would do and then work that into the fun. They swim, they wriggle their fins, they eat, they float—all things I could have the kids pretend to be doing while I finished my work.

I could hear them chatting about how they wanted to keep playing the game after lunch. They started to add to it in such creative ways, and I let them run with it. The older kids made an underwater world in our schoolroom with construction paper and tape. They gathered any sea-like toys or home decor they could find and let their imagination run wild. That simple reset activity that I was just using to try to calm them down so I could put away the groceries turned into a three-day-long adventure.

And I got a nap.

Your simple assignment:

1. From the following list (or using your own imagination), pick three ideas that will give you a do-over.

2. Build an arsenal of verses and quotes that encourage you, and put it in your phone, on your calendar, or on your fridge.

3. Straighten one small area of your home that has been bothering you. (Keep it minimal by just doing part of a drawer or one end of your dresser.)

4. Read Deuteronomy 11:18–25.

TWENTY IDEAS TO GET YOUR LIST STARTED (THESE ARE JUST FOR MOM)

1. Take a deep breath. It always helps.

2. Use essential oils. There are some amazing ones for calming your nerves.

3. Drink some herbal tea.

4. Take a shower. Even a quick one can calm you down.

5. Read a book or a magazine article.

6. Doodle. Doodling always calms me down.

7. Exercise, even if it's just for five minutes.

8. Listen to soothing music. I like music that incorporates the sound of water.

9. Make a date to have dinner with a friend. Just looking forward to it will help.

10. Pray for someone else.

11. Lie on the floor and stretch.

12. Have a cleaning race with the kids. Everyone cleans up as fast as they can for three minutes.

13. Fix something, just one thing, that's been bugging you. I always have a stack of broken toys and books with torn pages and other things the kids are waiting for me to do. When I need to feel like I've accomplished something, I fix one of them.

14. Wash one window.

15. Close your eyes and picture your children as adults; then pray for their future.

16. Scratch your back with a back scratcher.

17. Massage your hands with lotion.

18. Write a note to the first person who pops into your mind, just to tell that person you care about him or her.

19. Take pictures of something you love.

20. Brush your teeth for two minutes.

CHAPTER 10

Breaking It Down

There have been days when I felt like I was managing an old-fashioned one-room schoolhouse. I had kids of all ages learning individual lessons, with a baby or two in the corner begging for my attention, and I dreamed of someone ringing a bell and sending the kids all outside for recess. #calgontakemeaway

One particular day the boys were in rare form. They poked at each other and stared at me with blank looks when I asked them to solve a math problem. I felt like I was pushing a cartful of bricks through the snow. Uphill. Both ways.

After thirty minutes of getting nowhere, I gave them a piece of paper and told them to draw me a picture while I went into the kitchen to do a little dinner prep. I needed to step away from the difficulty of homeschooling for a few minutes. Deep breath. I repeated to myself, "It's going to be fine. They will eventually grow up and leave home and hopefully know how to multiply by then."

I had planned to make a pot of soup for dinner and needed to chop the vegetables. As I found all of my ingredients and tools, I could hear the boys fussing in the next room. I started to chop the onions with more aggression than necessary.

Now, I don't know how it is for everyone, but onion chopping is especially difficult for me. I am so sensitive to the fumes that my eyes start to water before I even make my first slice. I have tried everything: candles, goggles, matches, freezing the onions, cutting under water. Nothing helps. So I just try to get it done as quickly as possible.

On this day as I cut the onions into small pieces and listened to my children fuss in the next room, I asked God to help me figure out how to get the boys to focus and understand this math problem. Just as I was calming down I heard a loud crash from the other room. Ugh!

Irritated, I didn't even stop to put my ten-inch-long knife down before I marched around the corner. "WHAT is going on in here? Why can't you boys just settle down?!"

I had not thought about the view from their perspective: a sudden appearance of crazy Mom, wielding a knife and bawling her eyes out. They looked at me in shock. "We are sorry, Mommy. We didn't mean to make you cry."

Huh? Cry? (Oh right … the onions.) I almost told them I wasn't crying about them; it was because I was chopping onions. But then I realized, *maybe* this was the answer to my prayer. I walked softly over to them, knife still in hand, and told them gently, "Boys, you need to get your math done and then we can all go play outside. I will set the timer for twenty minutes, and when it goes off we will check your work." I handed them each a worksheet. "And if you get it all done, we can stop for the rest of the day."

I turned and went back into the kitchen to finish my veggie chopping. No sounds from the other room. I peeked around the corner. They were scribbling away on their papers. They were six and eight at the time, and I'm not sure which motivated them more, the tears streaming down my face or the knife blade.

RESET BY AGE

Every age has its sweet spot. Babies like to be rocked, but that doesn't work so well on my teens (not that I haven't tried ... they just won't get in my lap). Zoo games aren't fun for the older kids, and catching a ball is too hard for the little ones. As their maturity and needs change, so does the activity we use to reset a hard day. We're about to get into a few practical reset ideas for each age. I haven't given specific ages, as many of these principles will cross over. You know your child best, so read through the whole list and see what sparks your attention.

Babies/Toddlers

Babies can be so much fun, but when they get fussy, it feels like every man for himself. We have all experienced the mystery cry that persists, even after you've tried everything you know to do.

The key to getting through these difficult moments is to remain calm. If you get upset and high-pitched, they will have a harder time settling down. You set the tone and hold on to that. I sometimes have to talk to myself (in my head, of course): "Stay calm ... he is okay ..." and that helps. It can also help for me to focus on something in the room instead of the crying baby. Look at the pictures in the room, make a mental to-do list for tomorrow, anything to keep your heart rate steady and not let yourself get worked up.

The ideas that follow may not stop the baby from crying. Remember, you can't control everything; you can control only how you react. You are teaching your children, even at this young age, how to turn their upset moments into joy.

With babies, you need ideas that don't require them to participate. They can't copy you or follow instructions, so you need simple ways to divert their attention and show them how to relax.

So here are twenty ideas for the littlest ones in the family:

1. Spin around and around while holding them.

2. Take off all of their clothes (nakedness is freeing).

3. Wrap them tightly in a blanket or towel.

4. Whistle a tune.

5. Show them bright pictures.

6. Walk outside.

7. Give them a quick bath.

8. Snap your fingers while singing a simple song.

9. Rock in a rocking chair.

10. Blow bubbles.

11. Carry them like you're a pony (either by holding them or by putting them on your back).

12. Put their feet in warm water and let them kick around.

13. Let them play with your hair.

14. Imitate different animal sounds.

15. Throw a ball into the air and catch it over and over.

16. Shake a coin purse.

17. Let them listen to your earbuds.

18. Rub their legs gently from hip to foot (always going away from the heart).

19. Make up songs with their name in it.

20. Get a wet sponge and let it slowly drip on their hands.

Young Kids

Once they get a little older they can participate more in the do-over. It can be a lot of fun to add purpose to their playtime by showing them how to turn a grumpy attitude around. They can repeat after you, follow instructions, and perform simple actions.

But let me add that this is not about forcing anyone to participate. Sometimes they aren't going to want to play the game with you. That's okay. You just do it anyway and be sure they see what a good time you are having. This is about *you* stopping in the middle of an out-of-control situation and changing the focus. Even if you're putting on more of a show than playing a family game, it will still work. You're helping them learn that they can stop before they get into a total meltdown and turn the moment around. It reinforces trust in God and trust in Mommy and Daddy and shows them that you believe it when you say everything is going to be okay.

One important trick at this age is to be in their frame of vision. No yelling instructions from the other room. You will have to actually get up and move to where they are. Squat down, sit on the floor, or bend over and make sure they can see your face. This is so, so important when dealing with young children, especially, because they don't always pick up every word of what you mean. They are focused on what is in front of them, so let that be *you*.

And be understanding if they don't respond the way you expect. If you tell them, "Pick up your toys," several times and they don't do it, go over to them, get into their view, and instead of repeating exactly, say something different: "Stand up." Then after they do that tell them, "Now go move that truck to its place on the shelf," and so on. Break it down, be cheerful, be energetic, be fun-filled.

I can't stress enough how precious these years are. It is so tiring and so hard to get grown-up tasks accomplished, and sometimes you wish it were over. Believe me, I know! But before you can say "poopy diaper" it will be gone. I have no more babies. No more silly toddlers to cheer me up, no more all-night nursing sessions, and I MISS IT! I never thought I would when I was feeling so exhausted from it, but I really do. I am so thankful that I allowed myself to stop and enjoy my children and taught myself how to reset instead of losing my cool every time things didn't go my way.

Here are twenty ideas for turning around a rough day with younger kids:

1. Sing a silly song.

2. Dance around the table.

3. Flap like a bird.

4. Make alien noises.

5. Fill the sink with water and splash your hands in it.

6. Fill a pan with dry rice and run your fingers through it.

7. Turn on a fan and stand in front of it.

8. Flip the light switch on and off like a disco (let them do it too).

9. Lie in the grass or roll around.

10. Jump up and down saying, "HA!" with every jump.

11. Have a pillow fight.

12. Do jumping jacks (I love watching little kids do jumping jacks).

13. Lie on the couch with your head hanging off the edge.

14. Stomp around.

15. Toss a ball outside.

16. Draw your lipstick on really exaggerated to make yourself look clownish (let them do it too).

17. Hold your hands as high in the air as you can.

18. Act like dogs and cats.

19. Draw something funny. Color a picture of a purple sun or an orange ocean (we're going for easy here), and have them color it with you or draw their own.

20. Hop. That's it. Young children love to hop.

Older Kids

Then they get older, and oh, it is such a wonderful time! The world begins to open up, and they can explore more on their own and can be such a help to you. They are building skills and discovering their own gifts and talents and setting themselves on their life's path. It's a beautiful thing!

These kids still need you to get on their level when you are telling them something important. Not only does it help them follow your instructions, but it also helps you stay connected with them. Look them in the eye, touch their shoulder, and make real contact.

By now they should have some real responsibilities and be able to make some decisions on their own. This is a time for us to equip our kids with their own set of "tools" and help them build an arsenal for themselves. Memorize Scripture together, ask them to help you find ways to reset a hard day, and have them make their own list of ways to flip a difficult moment upside down.

No one can have a great day every day, and kids need a way to understand how to react when circumstances don't go as expected. For example, if Susie planned to go to her friend's house for the afternoon and it didn't work out, she will be really sad and possibly angry. She needs to learn how to respond in a way that is respectful and kind. If you have been doing resets with her, she knows how a quick burst of fun can help her feel better. So help her make a list of reset ideas to boost her mood when she is disappointed. Playing with her favorite toy, drawing a picture, singing her favorite movie theme song—there are so many ways she can reset by herself! Of course we want her to share her frustration with us; we care about her. But she should not take too long to recover from the disappointment, and a good do-over is a great way to get past it!

Kids in the older age range also need to feel like their place in the world is valuable. Give them some freedom to reset in their own ways. Talk with them about what they are feeling when they struggle to be nice/patient/helpful and how they can overcome that. A slow, deep breath is just as good for them as it is for you!

Make sure you are giving each child at least a few minutes of one-on-one time each day. It doesn't always have to be a long dinner date to satisfy their need for time with you. Just a couple of minutes talking straight to them and not being distracted is all they need under normal circumstances. Then look for opportunities to ask them how _____ is going (whatever you know is important to them). They need to know they are important and valued. They will learn to respect your ideas if you respect theirs.

These kids will be able to add activities to your list, but here are twenty things to get you started:

1. Play air guitar.

2. Dance with a broom.

3. Count backward (where to start depends on their age).

4. Point to each child and call out a category (movie, book, animal, etc.) and have them yell an example as loud as they can.

5. Stand on your heads against the wall.

6. Play patty-cake using your own songs.

7. Tear up a newspaper and throw it all over the ground (then play a clean-up game).

8. Call out shapes and have them find them around the room by running to them and touching the shape.

9. Play pretend drums on the table.

10. Have a sword fight with sticks.

11. Try to jump in a complete circle with one jump.

12. March around the house in a line. Call out objects they have to run and touch and then get back in line.

13. Say all of your grandparents' whole names with your tongue sticking out.

14. Walk around the outside perimeter of the house without bending your knees.

15. Put chairs from one end of the house to the other and walk across the house by stepping only on the chairs.

16. Walk around the house backward.

17. Run around outside acting like birds for five minutes.

18. Dump out a box of cereal (or chips, Goldfish crackers, pretzels, etc.) on the table and eat using only your mouth (no hands).

19. Clap in a pattern and have the kids repeat it.

20. Roll from one end of a room to the other.

Teenagers

And now we get to ... *dun-da-dun-dun!* ... the teen years.

This time in life is so full of angst and confusion and hormone surges and passion. It can be really, really hard to navigate. But it is so fantastic at the same time! As of this writing I have three children who have successfully made it through their teens, four currently in their teens, and two pulling up the rear. I am in the center of this hurricane and still hoping to come out alive.

Most days are filled with dealing with small, insignificant difficulties. But some days your teen just feels like screaming at the world, and you happen to be standing right in front of him or her when it hits. Don't take it too personally. While you shouldn't take abuse or accept ungodly behavior, let's give them some room to make mistakes and be inexperienced. I see this as an opportunity to gently guide them to an understanding of how to treat people, and I make an effort to not show them how hurt I am. They may feel like you are holding them back when really it's just nature. When my kids inadvertently hurt my feelings, I think to myself, *Just take it; you are the grown-up.* I try to remember what it was like to be fourteen and feel misunderstood. I assure my children they can trust me and we'll get through this together. I let them know I am here whenever they need me, even if I have to miss sleep. (And sleep is precious when you're old and exhausted; can I get an amen?!)

Some days I barely feel past the teen years myself, and I am so grateful for the grace I have been given.

One way to help snap a teen out of his or her pit of despair (name that movie) is by adding a bit of fun to the moment. The concept is the same as when they were younger, but the method is slightly different. As the needs change, the activities change.

When you notice that your teen is having a rough time (it's easy to notice; they're not subtle), you should stop for a minute and *listen.* "Hey, are you doin' okay?" or "I see that you are having a hard time today. Wanna tell me about it? I promise to just listen and keep my mouth shut."

I have three personal rules for myself when I am listening to my teens:

1. Don't interrupt.

2. Don't tell stories from my childhood.

3. Listen more than talk.

I may have advice for them, or I might even be slightly horrified at what they have shared with me. But I will keep that to myself until a later time. Or I might just offer a few quick ideas to help them feel hopeful but not give an entire sermon on their flaws. It's so, so vital that they feel they can trust you.

After they have told you whatever they want to say (sometimes nothing, and that's okay), stand up and suggest a good stretch. Exaggerate it. Stretch in their direction. Lean *way* over; be over-the-top about it. If you have teens who aren't outgoing, they may do it but with only half of the effort you give. So you have to go far beyond what you expect from them if you're going to get only half the result from them. And be joyful. There can always be joy even when it feels bad. Set that example for your teen. Maybe offer something you are glad about while you're stretching. Say something like, "This is a hard thing to go through, but I am *so* glad we have each other!"

Sometimes the situation calls for a double do-over. After you stretch and laugh, do another silly or unexpected thing. Here's a list of twenty ideas for teens (a lot of these will involve music; music does wonders!):

1. Learn one of their favorite songs, and then belt it out when they least expect it.

2. Read a few paragraphs of a great book (particularly one they love).

3. Try a new food, something you never thought you would eat.

4. Ask them to show you how to do something ... anything from skateboarding to playing the guitar.

5. Hold open a piece of newspaper and let them punch through it (do this several times).

6. Do crazy things with your hair (especially if you are going out somewhere).

7. Wear two different shoes.

8. Hold their hand (if they aren't opposed to it).

9. Dance around with your spouse. Teens need to see you loving one another.

10. Speak in a crazy accent.

11. In the car, play one of their songs as loud as you can stand it—with the windows down.

12. Throw a deck of cards in the air. When they land, whoever picks up the most face cards gets to choose the next meal (this is best done with just you

and one child so it doesn't become a competition among siblings).

13. Wear goofy glasses or Bubba teeth (I used to keep some of these in my purse).

14. Dance around to a rap song (there are some good Christian ones), doing your best gangsta moves.

15. Have a water gun fight.

16. Go outside and throw things (anything—rocks, sticks, leaves) for three minutes.

17. Make up moves to a favorite song and do them together to show Dad and the other siblings.

18. Shoot hoops, toss a ball, play Ping-Pong, or do something of that nature for just five minutes.

19. Trade shoes for an hour.

20. Do ballet (come on, you know you've always wanted to try it).

Moms, you can do this! It's not rocket science. It's just plain enjoying life. When life gets hard for you, it gets hard for everyone in the house. Even if the problem you are having has nothing to do with your kids, they still need to see you acting playful and having fun. If you've been sick for several days, on your first day out of bed plug yourself back in by doing some stretches with the kids and playing around for a few minutes. Look them in the eye. Smile. Give them encouragement that everything is going to be fine and they are a treasure.

And laugh!

Adding this kind of fun to a difficult moment is what makes life SO GOOD! Let go of your inhibitions and embrace the amazing things God is teaching you. You were built for this. You will make better lists than I could ever give you because yours will be so perfectly designed by YOU!

Use your chart with talents and plans and gratitude, and pull out all the arsenals you created, and you will be ready to turn the next hard moment into something that will change your family forever.

"DADDY ... WE MADE MOMMY CRY!"

That night after the crying-mom-wields-large-knife incident, we ate our soup. My husband always likes to ask the kids about their day during dinner, so when it came time for the boys to tell what their day was like, I braced myself. Would they give a report of a horror story, or would they show pride in getting all of their math done in under twenty minutes? These two were unpredictable.

I tensed up as one began to share, "Daddy ... we made Mommy cry!"

Oh dear. This may not go well.

My husband looked up from his soup and asked what happened. The boys gave a gripping report of how hard I was crying and the huge knife I was holding. When James asked them what they thought they did that made me cry, they said, "We finished all of our math work and she was so proud!"

Whuh?!

They didn't even remember it the way it actually happened. I had been so expressive afterward of how glad I was that they finished their math that they flipped it all in their minds.

And they were right!

I *was* proud of how they pulled it together. I was really happy that God answered my prayers in such a ridiculous way. I laughed later while they played outside, and my memories of the day were of joy and redemption.

I learned some lessons that day:

1. Kids are resilient.

2. Math problems can eventually be overcome.

3. Always have an onion on hand.

Your simple assignment:

1. Choose one idea from each list in the age groups that apply to you, and try it in the next three days.

2. Do something spontaneous. Surprise your family!

3. Read Psalm 37:4.

CHAPTER 11

Wrapping It Up with a Bow

On the second kitchen makeover, I made the regretful decision to paint some of my cabinets white. They looked so pretty for the first year or so. Then the slow deterioration began, and now they look like they were in a war zone: nicks and scratches and places around all of the knobs where the paint has completely worn off.

And yet … I love them so.

They make me happy. Those scratches were made by my kids as they learned to cook and did science projects. The worn-off paint is the result of little hands opening and closing the cabinets for years and years.

The little flaws tell a story of a family that eats together and works together and built a life together.

And that's what makes me happy. It isn't the perfect holiday meal or methodically organized pantry that makes life complete. It's the lessons we learn as we try to achieve those things. There's nothing wrong with wanting an organized pantry. In fact, I'm pretty compulsive about mine. But it becomes wrong when I have a tantrum because it gets messy or when I feel like it's a reflection of my entire life. It's just a pantry. You straighten it, they mess it up, you straighten it. Lather, rinse, repeat.

So why not enjoy the whole process? Why not embrace the continued efforts to work together and build a life? Why not laugh about it?

I'm not giving up on neatness and organization. I do think it's possible, even with a van full of little ones, to be on time to your planned activities most of the time. Embracing the hard times is not an excuse to let go of your efforts to improve. This is a way to not fall apart when things don't work out. You can still get things done and accomplish a LOT! I'm a get 'er done girl and I do pretty well. But there will always be glitches and obstacles. Always.

REMINDERS

Let's recap what we have learned. And feel free to refresh when you find yourself in a new time of struggle. As your needs change, you will find new ways to create that do-over you so desperately need by reading back through these chapters.

1. Know who you are. You are just the way God made you, and you have an amazing set of abilities that are unique to you. Don't be afraid to say what you are good at. It's wonderful to be around a person who knows what she is good at and uses those talents!

2. Remember your dreams. You are allowed to have dreams even though your life is already set on a path. You might change some things about your life, but more often you will alter your dreams to fit your life. But it's something so many of us lose sight of as we venture into the hard years of marriage and motherhood. Having our lives attached to other people can feel like a weight. But God tells us He created us beautifully and wonderfully, and He wants us to have a personal vision as well as a group one. Remind yourself of those dreams and unpack them into something you can still accomplish!

3. Identify your problems. It sounds so easy, but the truth is we need to dig deeper and see how we are contributing to our problems. Write them down, pull them apart, and think of one thing you can change about yourself, even if nothing else changes. If you can pinpoint where you are causing your own problems with poor attitudes or actions, then you can take the bull by the horns and achieve victory.

4. Connect the dots. We made a chart and connected our gifts and dreams to our problems. How can you use what God gave you to make your life better? Every talent comes with a multitude of opportunities. Soccer requires energy, precision, stamina, and sportsmanship. Those qualities can all be useful in problem solving! If you make quilts then you are likely great at design, coordination, detail work, patience, following patterns, and using your hands and feet at the same time. Wow! That's a lot of skill you've got there.

5. Make a plan. You know who you are and who your Maker is. You have a good idea of what your problems are and what skills you have to help solve them. Now make a solid plan. Write down what you think you might try, even if it feels silly. You can tear it up if it doesn't work and try something else. Tweak, adjust, but plan. Equip yourself with confidence!

6. Make changes. Don't be afraid to make changes in your life. We all need a do-over sometimes, and it's almost always up to us to make that happen. Instead of wishing for a winning lottery ticket to fall from the sky, start making small changes in the way you spend and how you think of money. Look to your talents to generate even a small amount of income and understand what you need to change to make an impact on your troubles. It's scary. It's not easy, but it's the road to the life you really want.

7. Find your JOY! This is essential to getting that do-over we all so desperately need. It sounds so simple—just three little letters—but it is *not*. Look to the Father of joy and He will pour it into you. Let Him wash away your fears and pain and insecurities and fill you with an everlasting, unexplainable joy that will permeate everything you do.

8. Practice. It's time to put our money where our mouth is. In the words of Yoda, "Do or do not. There is no try." (Wise words from a Jedi Master.) You must walk out your new plan and practice changing your responses to hard situations. Follow the five-step plan for getting started, and do it over and over again. You'll mess up sometimes, you'll learn, and you'll do better next time. Just do it.

9. Enjoy motherhood. This is the challenge of all challenges. But don't be fooled; it is also the most rewarding and is what God uses to make us more like Him. The trick here is to change your focus from perfection to enjoyment. It's time to add humor to your reactions. Yes, work on your tasks. Yes, build your dreams. *Definitely* build an arsenal of ways to inspire yourself. And, yes, let it all go when it doesn't happen exactly how you want.

10. Break it down. Take all you have learned and the courage you have built, and start adding humor. Be silly. Be flexible. Dance. Clap. Fall down laughing. Make yourself a list of ways to respond when days get hard so you are ready to solve your problems one moment at a time. Do it on a napkin at Starbucks if you have to!

Now that you have your chart, you can use this strategy over and over. Just keep chipping away whenever an issue comes along that you need to tackle. Then apply your plan and be ready to constantly reevaluate. Life isn't about being at the end; it's about getting there. And that means constant changes and shifts and moving ahead. Your problems today won't be the same ones you have in ten years (hopefully!), but your talents will be the same and you will be even better at them!

As for me, one thing I will do is repaint my kitchen cabinets pretty soon. Then they can tell a new story of a family that is working together to make home improvements and keep a clean house. There's always a story to be told. There's always a blessing to be seen.

What will your story be? That you yelled too much or got frustrated over little things? Or will your kids remember that you were unpredictable in your reactions and they never knew when you would blow?

I don't mind being unpredictable. In fact, I like it. But not because of anger. I want my kids to wonder what fun thing will come out of me next. When will I spontaneously stop what I am doing, pay attention to them, and add some playfulness to the day? They never know. It could happen at any moment.

PLAYING IT OUT

To help you move forward, here's a sample situation.

One morning you wake up feeling really grumpy. You've been up and down all night with crying children and a snoring husband. Your day is too full before it begins, and you aren't sure you will be able to pull this one off. People are expecting you to perform miraculous feats like being on time to your ladies' Bible study with a snack for your family and enough to share. You haven't done laundry in over a week, and your bank account is down to pennies. There's no time, no energy, no money, and your kids are already awake and calling out for you.

And to top it all off, you know that Mary-Perfect is going to be at the Bible study, and she will be all coiffed, and her kids will have on matching clothes that have been ironed, and her snack will be something you could find on Pinterest. She will even have recipe cards printed out and hand-decorated for everyone who begs to know how she made such a delightful snack. And you will want to hide in the corner with your saltine crackers topped with folded American cheese slices.

Now stop. Before you roll out of bed, take a long, slow breath. Hold it for a second before letting it out. Pray ... even a quick prayer. Ask God for strength and wisdom. Ask Him for a vision of joy and fun and to help you be a vessel for Him.

Just open your heart and mind to the possibilities, and let go of your own disappointment in what you are facing and how hard things are for you right now. Release yourself from feeling like a failure because you don't have that picture-perfect life you want.

Pray for Mary, pray for your husband, pray for your kids, and pray for anyone else you might run into today.

That whole action needs to take only a few moments. Then rise, go to the bathroom, and on your way, look up a few Bible verses on your phone. Or if you've printed some around your bedroom, read them and say them out loud to yourself. Be encouraged. Life isn't supposed to be easy. His Word assures us of that. You are right where you need to be.

As you get the kids up and make breakfast, take it slowly. Be cheerful. Find some fun little moments in the hustle to connect with them: feeding the baby, helping an older one wipe the table, teaching someone a simple lesson in tying shoes. When a mishap comes along (and it will!), stop and think before you react. Think about your child's needs, decide to figure out a solution to keep it from happening again later, and move forward.

One step at a time. Have the kids help you. Don't respond to whining. Make a mental list of what needs to be done before you leave the house (I even write it on our dry-erase board in the schoolroom). Then, one at a time, check things off your list. Stay cheerful. You're getting there.

As each moment passes and you get closer to your goal of leaving the house on time, look for ways to enjoy this day. Despite being tired and stressed and feeling insignificant, there is joy. There's joy in your weakness, there's joy in your children, and there's joy in the home you have, despite its imperfections. And have fun!

At least once, maybe while you get the kids bathed or dressed, play a little game to help you all focus. Have them name animals that start with different letters of the alphabet or have everyone walk on their hands and knees from the kitchen to the bedroom—including you. This will help them feel united in purpose and be able to enjoy the morning together.

Relax, Mom. You can get things done while maintaining an easygoing attitude.

Maybe before next week you will want to make a plan to get up earlier (which might require going to bed earlier) to make this weekly task easier. But for now, this is what you have. Pull together whatever snack you can, and don't be embarrassed about it. We have all been there. It's a season.

Now, to make the do-over complete, don't complain when you get to Bible study. Spend the time in the car on the way giving thanks for all you have, and look for the blessings of the morning. Let go of the bitterness over a husband who doesn't help or kids who won't move fast enough or a night of sleeplessness. Let go of your idea of what your life should look like. Find hope in making a plan to improve mornings like these in the future. Make it your mission to lift up the people you will see at Bible study. You can ask for prayer, but don't be whiny. (It helps me to think of people whom I find depressing to talk to and determine not to be like that.)

Going through life with a purpose to enjoy yourself right where you are is a beautiful gift—to yourself, to your family, to the lady behind you in line at the grocery store. Write it in your heart, practice it with confidence, and share it with others.

Go get that do-over, Mama!

Lisa's Black Bean Soup

*(This feeds a crowd, so if you have a small
family take some to a neighbor!)*

2 tbsp canola oil
1 1/2 onions, chopped
6 cloves garlic, minced
2 small green bell peppers, chopped
1 cup shredded carrots
3/4 tsp oregano
3/4 tsp thyme
2 tsp cumin
pinch red pepper flakes
6 cups chicken broth (I love Better Than Bouillon)
4 large cans black beans (drained)
salt and pepper to taste

In a large pot, heat oil over medium heat and add
onion, garlic, bell peppers, and carrots. Cook until
peppers and onions are translucent. DO NOT let

the garlic brown. Add spices and broth, and bring to a boil.

Add beans and bring back to a boil. Add salt and pepper.

Using a blending wand (you can do this by removing batches and putting in a blender if you don't have a wand), blend soup until about half the beans are pureed.

This is great with sausage added or topped with cheese or sour cream. Serve with corn bread and salad. Yum! Now I'm hungry.

Notes

Chapter 1

1. Angie Smith, *Mended: Pieces of a Life Made Whole* (Nashville, TN: B&H Books, 2012), 150.

2. Emily P. Freeman, *Grace for the Good Girl* (Grand Rapids, MI: Revell, 2011), 84.

Chapter 2

1. Jennie Allen, *Restless: Because You Were Made for More* (Nashville, TN: Thomas Nelson, 2014), 7.

2. Allen, *Restless*, 67.

3. Dave Ramsey, *The Total Money Makeover: A Proven Plan for Financial Fitness*, classic ed. (Nashville, TN: Thomas Nelson, 2013), 8.

4. Dave Ramsey, *Financial Peace Revisited* (New York: Viking, 2003), 30.

5. Bethany Hamilton, *Soul Surfer* (New York: Pocket Books, 2004), 54.

6. Allen, *Restless*, 202.

Chapter 3

1. Lysa TerKeurst, *Unglued: Making Wise Choices in the Midst of Raw Emotions* (Grand Rapids, MI: Zondervan, 2012), 32.
2. Shauna Niequist, *Cold Tangerines: Celebrating the Extraordinary Nature of Everyday Life* (Grand Rapids, MI: Zondervan, 2007), 178.
3. Elisabeth Elliot, *Keep a Quiet Heart* (Grand Rapids, MI: Revell, 2004), 25.

Chapter 4

1. Lysa TerKeurst, *Unglued: Making Wise Choices in the Midst of Raw Emotions* (Grand Rapids, MI: Zondervan, 2012), 113–14.
2. Jennie Allen, *Restless: Because You Were Made for More* (Nashville, TN: Thomas Nelson, 2014), 145.

Chapter 5

1. Candace Cameron Bure, *Reshaping It All: Motivation for Physical and Spiritual Fitness* (Nashville, TN: B&H Books, 2011), 40.
2. Shauna Niequist, *Cold Tangerines: Celebrating the Extraordinary Nature of Everyday Life* (Grand Rapids, MI: Zondervan, 2010), 148–49.
3. Elisabeth Elliot, *Keep a Quiet Heart* (Grand Rapids, MI: Revell, 2004), 82.
4. Laura Numeroff, *If You Give a Mouse a Cookie* (New York: HarperCollins, 1985), 2–4.
5. C. S. Lewis, *Mere Christianity* (New York: HarperCollins, 1952), 206.

Chapter 6

1. Thom S. Rainer and Art Rainer, *Simple Life: Time, Relationships, Money, God* (Nashville, TN: B&H Books, 2009), 73.

2. Lysa TerKeurst, *Unglued: Making Wise Choices in the Midst of Raw Emotions* (Grand Rapids, MI: Zondervan, 2012), 54.

3. Candace Cameron Bure, *Reshaping It All: Motivation for Physical and Spiritual Fitness* (Nashville, TN: B&H Books, 2011), 109.

4. C. S. Lewis, *Letters to Malcolm* (Orlando, FL: Harcourt, 1964), 26.

5. Dr. Henry Cloud and Dr. John Townsend, *Boundaries: When to Say Yes, How to Say No to Take Control of Your Life* (Grand Rapids, MI: Zondervan, 2008), 91.

Chapter 7

1. Elisabeth Elliot, *Keep a Quiet Heart* (Grand Rapids, MI: Revell, 2004), 91.

2. Elliot, *Keep a Quiet Heart,* 91.

3. Ann Voskamp, *One Thousand Gifts: A Dare to Live Fully Right Where You Are* (Grand Rapids, MI: Zondervan, 2011), 57.

4. Jennie Allen, *Restless: Because You Were Made for More* (Nashville, TN: Thomas Nelson, 2014), 43.

5. Jennifer Rothschild, *Self Talk, Soul Talk: What to Say When You Talk to Yourself* (Eugene, OR: Harvest House, 2007), 51.

6. Sheri Yates, *Stuck: Pull Your God-Given Dreams into Reality* (Edmond, OK: iKAN, 2013), 73.

Chapter 8

1. Emily P. Freeman, *A Million Little Ways: Uncover the Art You Were Made to Live* (Grand Rapids, MI: Revell, 2013), 138–39.

2. Lysa TerKeurst, *Unglued: Making Wise Choices in the Midst of Raw Emotions* (Grand Rapids, MI: Zondervan, 2012), 115–16.

Chapter 9

1. Shauna Niequist, *Cold Tangerines: Celebrating the Extraordinary Nature of Everyday Life* (Grand Rapids, MI: Zondervan, 2010), 177–78.

2. Lysa TerKeurst, *Unglued: Making Wise Choices in the Midst of Raw Emotions* (Grand Rapids, MI: Zondervan, 2012), 115.

3. Sheri Yates, *Stuck: Pull Your God-Given Dreams into Reality* (Edmond, OK: iKAN, 2013), 74.